Who do you say I am?

ALLAN TAVARES

ISBN: 978-93-5766-740-1

DEDICATED

To

My Novice Master

Fr. Mariano Dias, sfx

Who nurtured

my Love

for Jesus Christ

and sanctified me

by his holy life!

CONTENTS

ACKNOWLEDGMENTS

I am grateful to God and to my parents, my sister, my Godpa, and my grandparents for the gift of life and faith.

I am grateful to our Shubh Sandesh Gospel Echoes troupe, who inspire me with their love, enthusiasm, commitment, and passion to tirelessly cultivate the Gospel seeds through their talents of music, dance, and drama. They've given flesh and blood to the scripts.

I am grateful to my family, friends, and all my companions who have always stood by me.

I am grateful to all my students who unconditionally trust and confide in me and are ever -ready to support my Gospel ventures.

This book could see the light of day only because of Madison Hailey Fernandez, Alistair Tavares, Marcelino D'Costa sfx, Vanessa Castillo, Romeo Lopez, Victor Hernandez, and Janie Garcia, who motivated me and helped me to get my act together and get the book printed and publicized in Godspeed.

I am grateful to Fr. Vasant Ekka sfx for proofreading my book.

I am grateful to Fr. Marcelino D'Costa sfx for designing the cover.

PREFACE

Who do you say I am?

One of the things I have enjoyed most so far as a Priest is to incarnate my inspiration for a given liturgical season into a musical that could be staged for the public. This musical would eventually become a Gospel Echo. I call this passion my 'Shubh Sandesh Gospel Echoes' Apostolate.

'Who do you say I am?' – This question always rekindles me – A question from my Master. This book contains scripts of four musical plays. Each of these was written and staged as an attempt to answer my Master's question.

'Can I be a Messiah?' was staged in Goa in 2019, as an Advent reflection on Jesus of Nazareth as a teenager and an adult. It was set to music by Maestro Rev. Fr. Peter Cardozo, sfx. The cast was from Goa, Arunachal Pradesh, and Nagaland. Pilar Music Academy presented it under the leadership of Rev. Fr. Myron. Sequeira, sfx. One of the shows was infact on a stage in a lake in Durga (Goa).
''Emmanuel, but where is God?' was performed during the 2013 Christmas season at various old-age homes in Goa. The cast consisted of my students from Arunachal Pradesh.
'Are you there?' is a Lenten musical staged in Goa during the

Lenten seasons of 2018 and 2019. While we can be obsessed by the obvious fact of most of the apostles not being there at the foot of the cross, this musical imagines the apostles returning to the Calvary scene and, in a contemporary tone, also invites the audience to reflect on how much really are we there, accompanying Jesus when and where He needs us! It was set to music by Maestro Rev. Fr. Peter Cardozo, sfx. The cast was from Goa, Arunachal Pradesh, and Nagaland. Pilar Music Academy presented it under the leadership of Rev. Fr. Roncy Braganza, sfx. It was written as a bilingual presentation combining English with the native Konkani.
'Rise and Walk' is a Lenten cum Easter Musical. The Hindi version was staged in Bhopal (Madhya Pradesh). One of the shows was for a massive audience at the annual 'Easter Mahotsav'. The music arrangement was done by Maestro Rio Fernandes. The cast included the hostelites from Fr. Agnel Boys Hostel, Bhopal, and the 'Nishkalanka Girls Hostel, Bhopal, and the Religious and Parishioners of Pilar Mata Parish, Bhopal. Pilar Mata Parish presented it under the leadership of Rev. Fr. Agnel Bhoye, sfx.

The entire process of writing the script to directing each of these musicals and finally staging them has been a journey of deep bonding with the person of Jesus of Nazareth. Every member of our troupe felt immense joy in doing our little bit for our Master and for the proclamation of the Gospel.

We hand over the baton to you. God's grace will suffice you to bring these scripts alive again and make your love & joy abound as you unleash the Power & Peace of the Gospel to engulf every quark and quasar of our Universe.

- Minino Allan SMPTU Peter Tavares sfx

PLAY ONE

CAN I BE A MESSIAH?

The Characters

The first production of this play was at Pai Tiatrist Hall, Margao, on 1st December 2019, with the following cast:

GOD - Voice	Allan Tavares sfx
YOUTH 1	Trina Fernandes
REBECCA	Lania Laura Quadros
YOUTH 2	Ashwin Carlos Costa
LAZARUS OF BETHANY - Adult	
YOUTH 3	Patsmenia D'Costa
TERRORIST 1	Ignatius Noronha
JOHN	
TERRORIST 2	Roy Rodrigues
MATEUS - The Tax Collector	
TERRORIST 3	Seby Mendes
ALESSANDRO - The Centurion	
JESUS -Young	Sherwin Samuel Pereira
JESUS - Adult	Ronaldo Martinho Fernandes
MARY - Mother of Jesus	Sharon Barreto
JOSEPH - Father of Jesus	Trevor Barreto
SIMON OF BETHANY	Leslie Noronha
JOHN THE BAPTIST	
MARY OF BETHANY - Young	Kimora Barreto
MARY OF BETHANY - Adult	Lucy Tonglim
MARTHA OF BETHANY - Young	Arissa Paes
MARTHA OF BETHANY - Adult	Mevyia Rebello
LAZARUS OF BETHANY - Young	Cristo Afonso
REBECCA - Young	Lania Quadros
JAMES	Clayton Coutinho
CHOIR	Crescendo Cultural Group
DANCE TROUPE	Lemtam, Azilinda, Ritu, Ajonto, Elvis, Avinash

Concept, Script, and Direction by **ALLAN TAVARES** SFX

Music Composition and Arrangement by **PETER CARDOSO** SFX
Produced by PILAR MUSIC ACADEMY - GOA PROVINCE,
SOCIETY OF PILAR
TECHNICAL TEAM:
Movie Clips: **MANKAM**
Lights & Sound Effects: **LUIS**
Stage Marshal: **AJONTO**
Stage Managers: **ELVIS & LEMTOL**
Props Manager: **NILTON, NELIA, DEBBY**
Costumes & Make-up Manager: **SHARON & TREVOR**
Mike's Managers: **ANDREW & SAVIO**

The Troupe of 'Can I be a Messiah'

CURTAIN RAISER

Krist-ienneancho kall...umedin ani khaltikaien, Devacho ani eka-mekacho mog korun dhadoxi zaunk amkam apoita.
The Advent season is a call to find endless joy through selfless love.
Lenvtteponache tann'nent zori ami poddle zalear, ami monxank ani monisponnank valor dinanv....ami fokot poixank ollkotanv ani podven jieunk anvddetanv.
Poixeanchea ani Podvechea lenvtteponnnank lagun ami Deva sorlim pois zatanv ani eka-mekak tras ditanv.
Oslea patkantli....sodvonnenchi amkam goroz....ani soddvonnenchem kam - mhojem, tujem ani soglleanchem. Poixe, Podvi ani sogllo sonvsar zoddit ani otmo ibaddit zalear koslo laab mhaka?
Who will bring Peace, Compassion, Justice, and Joy to our craving and grieving human race?
We will need to be leaders who are a Messiah to one another!
How did Jesus and his friends respond to the call of being a Messiah in the troubled history of Israel?
Can I be a Messiah? Maybe I can.... Maybe I should! Let's sit and find out how we possibly could!

Scene one

A movie clip shows faithful, adoring baby Jesus at Christmas time.

This scene shows three youngsters in conversation with God while the carols and the movie clips unfold the drama of Christmas

[*The choir on stage sings*]

SONG 1: (CAROL) –
O Come, all ye faithful

REBECCA: (In Poetic Style)

Hi Folks! so good indeed to see thee....and me.... I am Rebecca....yes, Rebecca....simply Rebecca
You can think of me as a little girl who grew up with Jesus as a kid!
Maybe his neighbour...and his friend from the next street.
Then I can tell you something about Jesus, which, if you imagine, you will find true.
Jesus....the boy whom all girls loved to be with, was a happy boy of our neighbourhood.
Jesus' eyes sparkled with truth. His smile was attractive, and we liked what he said! He was the happy boy of our neighbourhood.
Jesus shared with us ideas...so creative.
We loved his ideas that were so funny yet big!
He got us to do things that made our parents happy.
Yes indeed, Jesus was the happiest boy of all our families

***Youth 1*:** O God! What was that?
Some Rebecca....who said she grew up with Jesus!
Jesus....she said, was the happy boy of her neighbourhood and of all their families

***Youth 2*:** Yes, I do agree that Jesus, even today, is the cause of Happiness for millions of families.

***Youth 3*:** Well, that's why Christmas is a happy time for the world. We celebrate Joy at Christmas

***Youth 1*:** But...just a thought.....Can we human beings ever be happy? Does the kissing of Baby Jesus really bring me to Peace?

***Youth 2*:** Or are we mere puppets on a stage, with you.....O God.... holding our strings?

***Youth 3*:** Hoi! sang Deva...Monis koso hanv khoreaninch asunk xoktam khuxal?.

GOD: OH, my girl.... time and again, you choose to throw me...in your frying pan

***Youth 3*:** Hey....I hear some voice...Could it be God?

GOD: Yes...this is your God speaking...and I said....time and again, You choose to throw me...in your frying pan. But please don't light the fire, 'coz in your fire I fry not .....I freeze!

Tum Devak Devuch zaunk dina zalear tujea jivitacher asa koslo hok mhaka?

***Youth 1*:** You have not answered my question.... have you? Your answers...anyways...I seldom understand

But how do you freeze in my frying pan?

***Youth 2*:** Well, you remain God, whether I choose to live or not like a man!

Youth 3: Tum Dev to Devuch....unnem kednanch zauncho nam!....punn hanv tor tuzo rupkar zalear, kuxal kiteak hanv aso nam?

Youth 1: I think we should return to that lively mood that Judith....reminded us of......I choose to live happy...... in total celebration!

GOD: That's a good choice, children! Living joyfully by

choice....is the right plan!
Monxea....zaum di tujem jivit mhojea sarkem, ek git....mogachem....kuxalkaiechem!

DANCE 1: DANCE OF JOY - Life as a celebration!

(courtesy: Microsoft Co-Pilot)

A movie clip, showing different expressions of happiness of individuals and communities beyond barriers of caste & creed

(enter three masked terrorists who yell and speak while the dancers continue

to dance on mute music)

TERRORIST 1: Stop all of it! You have no right to be happy!
To be desperate...is what I've chosen to be!
and being sad and gloomy ...is what I want your world to be!

TERRORIST 2: Mhojea jivitak....nam orth....nam rong!
Tumchea -i jivitachem hanv kortolom nisontonn!
Tumchea -i jivitachem hanv kortolom satyanas!
(*laughs as they shoot those on stage*)

TERRORIST 3: (*Talks to the audience*)
Ham....tum pe gholi nahim marenge.....hum aap logom ko lalach aur niraxa ka xikar bana denge.....aur tum kudd ek dusrom se laddte....laddte marenge..... (*laughs)*

A movie clip, on slow music, showing different expressions of terrorism..... Sound of a blast.....light effects on stage....as all the dancers are seen fallen on the ground with pensive music in the background.....choir moves back on stage (Choir members act as a crowd that gathers and assists in carrying dead bodies to the ambulance)

Youth 1: O God! Is this what you want? If you are God, then why do you let this happen?

Youth 2: Why should evil reign? Why do you allow the death of innocents?

Youth 3: Osle niropradi log morta tednam...zata Deva tum Khoxi? If you really want us to be happy, then why don't you stop such terrorists!

GOD: Monxea tujem jivit choloupacho odhikar, Tuvem mhojea hatantlo kadun ghetla. Tujem jivit tunch cholounk anvdeta. Tor ho tuzo vichar...kiteak mhaka?
You thank me not when content but complain when in pain. If being happy were by your own merit, why should your sadness be only if I permit?

Tuka hanvem....mhozoch rupkar koso rochla,
punn tum moluch dina.....monxak vo monisponnank.

Youth 1: But you can certainly intervene. You are God!

Youth 2: You should be in complete control of my life.

Youth 3: Tum Dev mhonntokoch odhikar asunkuch zai tuka! You are God after all!

GOD: Have you ever thought, why some child of mine...chooses to be so terrible...and whom you call a terrorist!

A terrorist is nothing but an extreme reflection of what becomes of you and of anyone...when you are selfish and ungrateful!

Tujem mon bodlop toddeach tempachem.

That's how you sound at every retreat, where crocodile tears roll down your cheeks. You make promises that you never keep!

Youth 1: But...You are God!

Youth 2: You can overrule it all!

Youth 3: Tum Dev mhonntokoch...Dev koso dakhounk zai Tuvem!

GOD: Yes indeed, I overruled it all and therefore inspite of Israel's waywardness, as God....I chose to be a human being born of a woman - a complete man of flesh and feelings. I wanted to see if being ungrateful, proud, and selfish was so compulsory as you make me think!

Hanvem ghetlem monxachem soimb, zannam zaunk....patok monxak kiteak itlem sotaita tem!

Youth 1: But... God!...with due respect, may I ask: What difference did you make, born as a man?

I know you lived well.......happy as Judith said...

Youth 2: But in your name, they've started just another religion! Was that your intent: To add another ingredient to this pot of confusion?

Youth 3: Tum monis zaun....fokot anink ek dhorm ailo rochun!

Ani sogllech dhorm mhonttat....Tum tancho Dev.

GOD: Well....I think....while all the rest of my creation has always been obedient. The one whom I created as my own reflection has always missed the point.
Hanv monis zal'lom , jikunk monxak mhojem sovem
Hanv monis koso jieunk paulom monisponnan, Mhojea avoi-bapaichea borea dekhik lagon

Yes, I raise a toast to my parents, Mary and Joseph.
for they raised me...a simple village child as a beloved son of God

[*The choir on stage sings*]

A movie clip shows Angel Gabriel appearing to Mary and then later to Joseph, announcing the birth of Jesus

SONG 2: (CAROL) - O Holy Night!

GOD: Wake up, O kids! I love your questions! Tell me now: would any one of you want to be a Messiah...a Saviour, in your world of sin and chaos?

Youth 1: God! I understand not, what you say!

Youth 2: How can I be a Saviour?

Youth 3: Hanv ek sadhem tornattem! Sodvonnechem kam hem ek vegllench apounnem!

GOD: Hoi dhuve mhoje......Vaitt sonvsarant zata mhonn fokot bobatt marpachem kam tujem ani tem vaitt poisaunk tuka hanv vinchun kaddunk soddtam tednam...tum mhaka sangta...tem kam mhonn anink konnachem...nhoim tujem.... Children...watch the lives of Joseph and Mary. Simple and young as you are, they are perfect examples of lives so true. They rekindled the gift of God within me, their son, amidst chaos and crisis that brewed!

With patience and kindness, they nourished me. With humility, they set me free.

Marian ani Juzen, aplem boremponn, mhaka tanchea bhurgeak - Jezuk dilem. Deivikponn, monisponnachea aidonnant mhaka jevoilem

Youth 2: God! Can you help me see it more clearly?

[*The choir on stage sings*]

A movie clip shows Joseph and Mary searching for a place at the inn...denied, Mary gives birth to Jesus in a manger....also shows the shepherds and the wise men from the Orient coming to the manger to worship Him

SONG 3: (Konkani CAROL) - Xant Nixa

Scene Two

A movie clip, showing Jesus, Mary, and Joseph at the Jerusalem Festival....and Jesus lost and found in the Temple.
The scene is at Nazareth, home of Jesus, where they are visited by their friends from Bethany

[*Mary in prayer*]

[SONG 04: He's doing His Father's business]

MARY: Abba, my Living God
Our Jesus got lost
at his first Passover in Jerusalem.
I was quite scared, remembering
how Herod wanted to kill him,
and killed so many innocents when Jesus was born
And lo, Jesus was bothered not.
He was discussing with the elders, his thoughts
of what he had learnt about you at our synagogues
about you as a Living Loving Almighty God

Deva mhojea!
Mhozo Put mhaka sangta
tannem khand marla khoim kamank...tachea Bapachea.
Zaum mhojea puta sovem O Deva
tujeach ieuzonne pormonnem

[*Enters Joseph, with Simon from Bethany, along with his three children, Mary, Martha, and Lazarus, who were of Jesus' age*]

JOSEPH: Mary, see who is here! Our friend Simon from

Bethany, along with his two beauties, Mary, Martha, and their brother Lazarus.

MOTHER MARY: Simon, I am blessed to see you again! Please come in....*(Takes them to the fireplace)* This is your home as much as you make us feel at home at Bethany! We were just talking the other day about how much you helped us during our visit to Jerusalem....and especially when our naughty son got lost in the temple.....(turning and hugging the kids)....and these three angels became such good friends of our Jesus.

[Mary washes and wipes their feet]

LAZARUS: Where is Jesus?

JOSEPH: I'd seen him running out with Rebecca! I'll find him out.... *(calls out to Jesus)*

[Mary serves them water to drink]

JESUS: *[comes running in with Rebecca]* Uncle Simon! Thank you for coming......thankyou for bringing Lazarus, Mary, and Martha.....

MOTHER MARY: Where were you, son? Where did you run out with Rebecca?

JESUS: Mother ....there was a Samaritan traveller who fell in a roadside ditch...I saw him...and Rebecca and I helped him with some water from our well!..... Hey, my Bethany buddies.... I was missing you like crazy. How have you been? Please meet Rebecca, my friend from our neighborhood! *[They greet one another]*

REBECCA: Jesus told me about the great time he had with you in Bethany! You look so friendly!

JESUS: What can I serve you?

MOTHER MARY: Jesus was in the kitchen today. *(to Jesus)* I was wondering why you prepared the broiled fish...before you ran out.... maybe you knew they were coming!

JESUS: *[laughs loudly]*You see, Mother, I am truly busy about my Father's business, so he gives me ideas! *(to the guests)* Yes, I will serve you what I prepared myself.....broiled fish in olive oil!.... Mother has also prepared some oven-baked bread to be eaten with pure honey spread! We also have some good figs from our neighborhood

MARTHA: You prepared the fish yourself?

REBECCA: Yes, Jesus is a great cook!

MOTHER MARY: Yes, Martha! He also knows how to roast the lamb in herbs! You may find it at the table tomorrow! He is good at everything....including mischief!

JESUS: Mother.....when you appreciate...do it completely....When I don't play mischief....you miss it so badly....hanv mostio korinam zalear, tujem thondd zata lamb....*(Jesus runs...as his mother runs towards him)*

MOTHER MARY: Alright ....I know you can run faster than me now....come....serve the food!

MARTHA: I could help you, Jesus.

JESUS: Yes, please, let's do it together. *[all the kids under Jesus' supervision and under Mother Mary's watchful eye serve the food] [Joseph serves wine to Simon as they chat in their corner....Mother Mary leads them to pray...and then all begin to eat]*

SIMON: Joseph, were you able to confirm about Jesus' further studies in Jerusalem?

JOSEPH: Yes, Simon, I took Jesus to the Hebrew Academy at Jerusalem, and he is supposed to be joining there in another year or two. But this little teenager has some ideas of his own! He wasn't really so keen on it!

SIMON: But your son is damn intelligent! His questions are from all over the universe! Do you remember when you returned from Jerusalem, how disturbed Jesus was by the sacrificial offerings at the temple? He was asking why the Heavenly Father needs the slaughter of so many innocent and helpless animals.

JOSEPH: Yes, he asked that often!

SIMON: And what do you answer?

JOSEPH: I choose to be silent....I know.....His questions can be very embarrassing, too! All said and done! He is a fine lad....so loving...lovable....and has begun learning my trade! He is already a handy helper at work!

[*The kids finish their meals, and Jesus animates them into some action song*]

JESUS: Lazarus, do you remember the clap song we composed at your place in Bethany?

LAZARUS: Yes, I do!

JESUS: .... Mary gave us some nice dance actions for the song! *(Mary blushes)* Mary, could you lead us to dance and sing?

MARTHA: Yes, Mary....we can be ourselves here...this is like home! and Rebecca....do you know the song?

REBECCA: Jesus taught all of us your 1-2-3-4 song - after he returned from Bethany....and he was praising Mary for her good dance steps....

MARY: But they were your words, Jesus....So, you sing.....I act & dance....and then we all do it together!

ALL: Agreed!

[SONG 05: A CLAP FOR GOD OUR FATHER]

JESUS & MARY: 1-2-3-4....Clap for our God

Clap for our God...our Loving Father.
Living....Loving...Almighty God
Creator...Protector...provides for all!

ALL: 1-2-3-4....Clap for our God
Clap for our God...our Loving Father.
Living....Loving...Almighty God

Creator...Protector...provides for all!

JESUS: Suria...chondrim...akash...
soglIo Devan kela.
Uzvadd...kallok...zomin...
soglli tannench vanttlea
Ghotto...tandull...fulam...
pormoll tannench rochla
Udtea musak...ranant vagak....
Devan posla
Bhavam Bhoinnimnom,
novem git gaiat
Sorgar...prithumer...Devak vakhannat
Bhavam Bhoinnimnom,
novem git gaiat
mogan tachea sogllo sonvsar rochat

ALL: 1-2-3-4....Clap for our God
Clap for our God...our Loving Father.
Living....Loving...Almighty God
Creator...Protector...provides for all!

JESUS: Mai....choilem mhunge...Mary kit nachot tem! solid! Khastachem!.... Mary! You dance so well!

MARTHA: I, too, dance well, Jesus!

JESUS: Yes..Yes, you too dance well, Martha!.... We all dance well! Let's do it again

ALL: (SONG 05): 1-2-3-4....Clap for our God
Clap for our God...our Loving Father.
Living....Loving...Almighty God
Creator...Protector...provides for all!

Hurray!

(Mother Mary serves them Grape juice.....they all run and grab their share)

LAZARUS: We missed you so much after you left Bethany. We were also trying to understand what your mother said to us!

JESUS: What was it, Mother?

MOTHER MARY: I was telling them what you said to us when we found you at the temple.

JESUS: What did I say!

JOSEPH: Son, you said to your mother that the hour has come for you to begin to be about your Father's Business!

MARTHA: Who is your father...?

JESUS: My Mother told me that I must be a beloved son to a Living...Loving...and an Almighty God....She taught me to pray to him, like this:

(Jesus sings...first four lines)

Mhojea Bapa sorginchea
Tujem nanv povitr zaum
Tujem raj amkam ieum
Tuji khuxi sorgar zata
toxich sonvsarant zaum

MARY: And that makes our God.....a Loving Father.

LAZARUS: Are we not too young to think about all this?

JESUS: I am thirteen. We have already studied at our synagogues...We are confirmed Jews. We are no longer babes in faith!

MARTHA: So, what about the Father's Business? What are your plans?

REBECCA: Jesus always asks questions to our Rabbi during the instructions at the Synagogue.

MARY: Jesus, we want to hear more from you.....

LAZARUS: And you can trust us... in case you need a helping hand with your Father's Business?

JESUS: There is so much hatred everywhere....we Jews hating the Samaritans....and they hating us!.... The Romans ruling over us....and we hating them....We need a Messiah!

MARTHA: Who is a Messiah?

JESUS: Messiah is a Saviour...sent by God to save God's people.

LAZARUS: How to be a Messiah?

JESUS: I think...we can learn to be a Messiah from our parents... My Father... simple...hardworking...is totally committed to taking care of the family. My Mother told me how he saved me from being killed by the king! He is the best carpenter in town, but never proud nor greedy.... and My Mother is full of grace...and compassion.. she has taught me to pray and ponder. She always tells me not to have any enemies. She says I must immediately forgive anyone who tries to harm me, because they know not what they do.

MOTHER MARY: (to Jesus) Son...do you know and understand what you are saying!

JESUS: Not really! I am telling them what you so often tell me....But I have learnt to forgive. I forgave one of my colleagues who punched my nose at the synagogue....*(All laugh)*

REBECCA: Yes, Reuben was really mean....he made Jesus' nose look like a pumpkin!

JESUS: And I forgave him!

MARY: Our Father too is very caring and daring!.... So, he too is a Messiah!..... And he loves your family.

MARTHA: So, to be a Saviour isn't impossible....we can learn from our parents to be a Messiah.

LAZARUS: Hurray! My Father is also a Messiah!

SIMON: Look at our kids....they talk so big!

JOSEPH: They search for truth in the eyes of their parents.....and the truth sets them free to fly beyond our reaches!

MOTHER MARY: Fly they must....to receive graces from

above... and from their flight to truth and goodness will our world benefit indeed!

JESUS: *(to his Mother)* Mother, what do you say? Can I be a Messiah? *(Mary interrupts)*

MARY: Jesus, can you show us your fig trees?

JESUS: Yes...come...I'll take you there!

[*The choir on stage sings*]

SONG 6: (CAROL) - Sang kiteak ailai Balla

DANCE 2 (on Song 6) - DANCE OF INCARNATION - Word became Flesh!

(Courtesy: Microsoft Copilot)

Scene Three

A movie clip, showing the political situation of Jesus' time, while the choir sings.

[*The choir on stage sings*]

SONG 7: (CAROL) - Tarka ie begin...begin

The scene is at Bethany, home of Mary, Martha, and Lazarus. Mary is in bed, not keeping too well, and Martha is cooking lamb specially for Jesus, who is their guest and is expected to return from Jerusalem. Lazarus is attending to Mary and assisting Martha. Fatima, a neighbour of theirs, is dancing to some traditional music to regale her friend Mary.

DANCE 3 - DANCE OF HEALING - Friendship heals!

(Courtesy: Microsoft Copilot)

Everyone is enjoying the graceful dance movements of Fatima. Mary finds vibes of health and wholeness in Fatima's dance gestures. Everyone applauds Fatima as she winds up her dance of friendship.

FATIMA: Mary, get well soon. I'll see you later.

MARY: Thank you, Fatima.

MARTHA: Mary, please have the soup that Lazarus is serving you while it is hot...you should be feeling fine soon.

MARY: I will be completely fine when our Jesus is back home.

LAZARUS: Yes, he should be back by evening. He said he would catch up with his cousins in town.

MARTHA: Mary...tell me something....Are you in love with Jesus?

MARY: Of course I am.....and I believe you too are. Who would not be in love with Jesus?

LAZARUS: Is he that handsome? More than me?

MARTHA: You too are handsome brother....there is something beyond the senses in Jesus!

MARY: I tell you....He glows in beauty. His eyes sparkle with Truth and Goodness! He is the one whom Israel is expecting!

LAZARUS: Mary....do you seriously think that Jesus is the chosen one...The Messiah?

[SONG 08: He is the Messiah]

MARY: Oh, yes, he is the chosen one
Who will lead us all to freedom
from suppression....oppression
And from our slavery to sin
Our Jesus is the Messiah
sent by God the Father
to show us the way
of Truth and Wisdom

MARTHA: Mary, you need to sleep...Lie down, please! *(Martha helps Mary lie down)*

MARY: I love him....but he can never be mine. My love for him will infact free me from the clutches of desire!

LAZARUS: Mary....you need to sleep!..... I can hear voices *(peeps out)* Jesus is back....I can see some men accompanying him! *(rushes out to receive them)(enters with Jesus, James, John, and John the Baptist - the cousins of Jesus)*

JESUS: I know....Martha is cooking lamb ...we all walked fast because the strong, delicious aroma of the lamb could be felt a mile away from here! *(Martha blushes)* And how is my Mary doing?

LAZARUS: She has just gone to sleep. While she was awake, she was all ga-ga about you. She even confessed that she is in love with you.

JESUS: What's the secret about that Lazarus? We were in love from the first time we met as teenagers.....When I say we....I mean you too, Martha! It's been a long time since we've known each other! We are all in our late twenties now. Hey, let me introduce you to my cousins.... James and John, sons of Salome, my mother's first cousin. and my mentor and cousin John, the son of Elizabeth, my mother's other first cousin.

MARTHA: And of course I know Mateus the tax-collector....what makes him hang out with you, Jesus?.....and well he seems to be accompanied by his Roman Boss....Jesus, you have a strange collection of friends!

MATEUS: Martha...I am sure you have enough reasons to hate me....but be assured, I will trouble you no longer!

JESUS: Yes, Martha, Mateus has chosen to give up collecting illegal taxes and has given away his ill-gotten wealth to the poor.

MATEUS:.... and yes...I want to hang out with Jesus...to find my own inner inspiration.

ALESSANDRO: I really admire your straightforwardness, O woman.

MARTHA: Friendship with Jesus...makes all genders equal and bold!

ALESSANDRO: and you find in him a rare connection with a Living and an Almighty God!...which I truly admire!

LAZARUS: Welcome, friends, to our little home at Bethany. Jesus is our family, and we would be happy to make you all feel at home....ofcourse Martha has prepared her best preparation of lamb for Jesus with some finest herbs and wine. I'm sure you all will like it!

JESUS: Oh yes.... Martha is a great cook...and we all are hungry....but before we grab our meal...let's complete the serious discussion that we were engaged in this morning!

LAZARUS: Oh what a discussion that was.....of how to end the messy socio-political situation of our times!

JESUS: Yes indeed! Let me summarize for the sake of my cousins!

[SONG 09: Israel, the chosen one]

JESUS: To begin with...let me say
Israel's history...is crazy
A living God...and unfaithful people
walking through the deserts of time....

Stories of Patriarchs: Abraham, Isaac, and Jacob
And Moses led the liberation from the Egyptians
Stories of successful self-rule under Hebrew kings
such as King Saul, David, and Solomon

A story of conquest and oppression
under the Babylonians, Persians, Greeks
And now the Romans
The story of Israel
always a victim seeking redemption

LAZARUS: So what do you want to do
This is what I asked you this morning
And you said there has to be a way
to everlasting freedom

JESUS: I can't be a zealot...for violence is not my choice
I can't be a Sadducee...
compromising freedom for status
I can't be a Pharisee...mere idealist spiritual hypocrite
I can't be an Essene...ascetic, cut off from society

And yet I can be all of it and more than that
If I find the House of my God in a mess.

I want to be His humble servant
I'd like to share compassion as his chief steward
I would also dare to be his sage and prophet
I'd love to be Shepherd of His flock!

JAMES: So...do you think you are the Messiah?

MARTHA: *(yells in panic)* Mary is gone cold! She is not responding! *(Martha cries loudly) (Lazarus rushes to her bedside and checks her pulse)*

LAZARUS: You need to do something, Jesus! I know you can.

MARTHA: *(yells out loudly)* Jesus, I know you will bring her back....I know how much you love her......and you must, because I know....You are the Messiah.

JESUS: Yes indeed! This is our moment! Let us be ready to worship God in Truth and Spirit!

We are all hungry and are eagerly waiting to eat the delicious lamb!

ALL: What?

JESUS: Hungry as we are....let us give up our meal tonight and sacrifice our desire. Let this fasting be our fuel as we raise our voices in prayer to the Giver of Life!

ALL: Yes, we shall!

JESUS: Abba Father! This is your moment of revealing yourself to us! You know how much Mary loves you. We need her right now because we are all seriously discussing how to save Israel.... your people! And for what our prayer alone can't do, kindly accept our fasting as our true offering! And I truly believe that when two or three of us are gathered in your name in sincere prayer and fasting, you are really present among them. So, I thank you, Abba Father...that you have heard me. *(Mary rises and sits on her bed) (Jesus gives her a hand)* Wow, that was great! Mary....how strong and true is your faith and love...and Our God does work His wonders to reveal to us what a Living...Loving and Almighty, a God He is!

LAZARUS: You are indeed the Messiah! You are the Way...the Truth and the Life that will set Israel free! *(Jesus gets Mary to drink some juice)*

ALESSANDRO: OH man, Jesus! Your God has given you authority even over death!

[SONG 10: The Messiah is a lamb]

JOHN THE BAPTIST:

Oh Yes! He is the chosen one!
Who will lead us all to freedom
From Suppression...from oppression.....
And from our slavery to sin! - (2)

Our Jesus! He is the Messiah...
Sent by God the Almighty Father
to show us the way...
show us the right way
of Wisdom & Freedom

I am not worthy! to untie his sandal straps
Yet he chooses to be humble
Meek & Humble! Simply Gentle!
A Beloved Son to God

JESUS: I think, to be a Messiah...is the call of a Nation...Each one of us is born as a unique manifestation of the Messiah

JAMES: Can anyone choose to be a Messiah.....and save our nation......?

JESUS: Tum monxakullak ani tujea desak sodoitolo zalear tujea Devacho niz mog tujea horddeant ani xiramnim asunk favo. We first pledge to love God with all our heart, with all our mind, with all our soul, and with all our strength.

MARTHA: And like Jesus, we pledge to love our neighbour as ourselves.

JAMES: Porjecho ani desacho Soddvonnar zatolo zalear.....podvechi, famad zaupachi vo poixeanchi axa asunk favo nam.....Hem mhojean korunk zatelem?

JOHN: Yes, we choose to be a Messiah not for power and status, not for revenge and to safeguard the law, not to remain aloof and preach platitudes...

JESUS: So John...what do you say: Can't you be a Messiah? James, kiteak zaunche nam tujem lagim zaunk niz soddvonnar he Devache porjek?

JOHN: Jezu tum mhozo ek apurbaiecho soiro....ani niz mog ani sasnnik ixtaggot hanv tuje xim xiktam....In communion with you, my Jesus...my cousin whom I love the most, I can certainly play my bit to rid our human existence of violence, sin, and disease!

JAMES: Devacho niz mog hanvuim kortam punn ghottaiechi mhaka goroz...zaunk Soddvonnar porjecho.

JOHN BAPTIST: You need to hear His voice in the wilderness.... to be His Voice of Salvation! You need to find time alone with the Alone to be the Messiah of your times!

JESUS: Each one of us is born to do this! We can't be so selfish as not to find time to spend with our Creator and understand his plan for our salvation!

You, my dear cousin John....have always dared to be different....Your life of penance and boldness is my inspiration!

JOHN BAPTIST: I am just a voice.... preparing the way...I am just a voice in the wilderness!

Sotan, mogan ani bollan, sodvonnechea kamank khand ami marum-ia!

JESUS: Voi! Asa hanv toiar, marunk khand soddvonnechea kamank! If my God willeth, then I am ready to be a Messiah......because I love my God and my neighbour.

MARY: Jesus....you need a team! You will be the Messiah indeed, and yet you need to live beyond your dream! Your dream then will live beyond your death and usher in a civilization of Compassion... Joy....and Peace!

JESUS: O my Mary...you've said it all!

MARTHA: We will never leave our Messiah alone!

LAZARUS: We truly relish our friendship with you, O Jesus. While my sisters have learnt to move from their crush on you to be your true soulmates, sensing your needs sometimes more than you do, me....lazy and never much expressive....would today want to declare from every housetop, that my best friend Jesus.....completely human....is so indeed human that I truly experience my living God... in him! Voi! Mhozo Jivo Dev mhaka hea monxachea, mhojea ixtta Jezuchea rupan disti poddta.....Niz monis zaun monisponnnan jieunk Jezu tum mhaka xikoita!

JESUS: O Lazarus, Martha, and Mary....you are such wonderful buddies....my soulmates indeed!

MARY: (sings) Jesus....you make me smile...I want to dance for the one who brought me back to life! (2)
lets dance to our friendship and to our merciful God!

JESUS: How wonderful these last few moments have been!
A bold proclamation of God's mercies and our eternal friendship! Yes! Let's dance with Mary and make up for Martha's roasted lamb that we've sacrificed!

[SONG 05: A CLAP FOR GOD OUR FATHER]

MARY: 1-2-3-4....Clap for our God
Clap for our God...our Loving Father.
Living....Loving...Almighty God
Creator...Protector...provides for all!

ALL: 1-2-3-4....Clap for our God
Clap for our God...our Loving Father.
Living....Loving...Almighty God
Creator...Protector...provides for all!

JESUS: Suria...chondrim...akash...sogllo Devan kela
Uzvadd...kallok...zomin...soglli tannench vanttlea
Ghotto...tandull...fulam...pormoll tannench rochla
Udtea musak...ranant vagak.... Devan posla
Bhavam Bhoinnimnom...novem git gaiat
Sorgar...prithumer...Devak vakhannat
Bhavam Bhoinnimnom...novem git gaiat
mogan tachea sogllo sonvsar rochat

ALL: 1-2-3-4....Clap for our God
Clap for our God...our Loving Father.
Living....Loving...Almighty God
Creator...Protector...provides for all!

[The choir on stage sings]
A movie clip shows Jesus' public ministry of preaching and healing!

SONG 11: (CAROL) - JOY TO THE WORLD

GOD: Where are you, O Kidos?
Jezuchea Jivitacher nodor martana
me'lla koslo tori nirop tumkam?
Did Mary, Joseph, and Jesus, with their bunch of friends, inspire you?

Youth 3: Yes! Mary, Joseph, and Jesus were so real, like me or like any of my fellow youngsters!
Youth 2: Mary, Joseph, and Jesus meant what they said and did!
Youth 1: Jesus and his young friends
built together a legacy

of being a Messiah
in Israel's troubled history

Youth 3: Jezu tornatto mhojea sarko....xiztel'lea rogtacho ani Soddvonnechea Kamank aplea ixttam sangatim khand tannem marlo....Jezu bhaxen sodvonnechem kam amkam tornatteank chalu dovrunk poddtelem!

Youth 1: But....Can I be a Messiah...Can I be a Saviour? Mhojea somazant zaunk xoktam hanv ek soddvonnar?

Youth 2: Maybe I can be a Messiah...Ghoddiek sotan, mogan ani bollan mhojea koxttovtolea bhavam-bhoinnank sodvonn haddppachem kam, mhojem, tujem ani soglleanchen...Maybe we should all give an honest try to be a Messiah to our times!

ALL: Seriously Yes! We can be a Messiah like Jesus or team up with the Messiah as his friends and relatives did! And that will indeed make us all eternally happy!

(All laugh their hearts out)

A movie clip shows contemporary acts of kindness, boldness, and wisdom

[SONG 12: Let me be....A Messiah]

Youth 1:

Our generation lives in pain and in disdain
knowing not what it seeks nor what it defends
We have dumped our dignity as children of God
and chosen to live in cages and prisons

CHOIR:

Can I be a Saviour
Can I live on the path of freedom
Can I lead my generation
to everlasting Truth and Goodness

Youth 2:

Jesus chose to live, doing His Father's business
He chose friends and mentors who helped him focus
He chose apostles and responded to his times
He chose to be a Messiah and led with wisdom

Youth 3:

Jezuchem jivit zaum-di dekh mhaka
Jieunk sotan, mogan ani xantikaien
Jezuchem jivit zaum-di dekh mhaka
haddunk nit ani dhadosponn mhojea somazant

CHOIR:

Let me be a Messiah
Let me live on the path of freedom
Let me lead my generation
to everlasting Goodness and Wisdom

Joy to the world! The Lord is come.
Let earth receive her King
Let every heart
Prepare Him a room
And Saints and angels sing
And Saints and angels sing
And Saints and Saints and angels sing

PLAY TWO

EMMANUEL, BUT WHERE IS GOD?

The Characters

The first production of this play was for the inmates of Nazareth Old Age Home, Navelim, Goa, on 15 December 2013, with the following cast:

Narrator	*Allan Tavares sfx*
EMMANUEL	*Kuman Kimsing*
LUIS – Emmanuel's Dad	*Mankam Mossang*
SWEETIE – Emmanuel's Mom	*Womkop Tonglim*
ANNA - Neighbour 1	*Baby Gurung*
SIMON – Neighbour 2	*Thantol Mossang*
MANJULA -Friend	*Gracy Gurung*
CATHERINE – Manju's Mom	*Roslyn Pinto*
BRUNO – Manju's Dad	*Phutang Mossang*
BERNARD - Friend	*Michael*
NIXON - Friend	*Jayanta Kumar Gogoi*
JUDE - Friend	*Soyo Wungsek*
	Devaiah Maditera,
CARLOS - Friend	*Michael Bimal Sorreng*
BASIL - Elderly	*Inmate*
LYNETTE -Elderly	*Inmate*
PEDRIN - Elderly	*Baby Gurung*
JOAO - Elderly	*Thantol Mossang*

Concept, Script, and Direction by **ALLAN TAVARES** SFX

(The Troupe of Emmanuel, but where is God?)

Scene 1

Celebration of a Newborn Babe at Christmas

It's Christmas day….and a day of double joy to the Dias family….after 14 years of long, patient waiting…they are blessed with a plump, healthy boy on Christmas day….The neighbours and relatives gather for a very special Christmas party with the Dias' family.
Youngsters carolling and having fun.

LUIS: And he shall be called Emmanuel….
SWEETIE: Yes indeed! Emmanuel indeed will our Son be…For God has been with us in this pretty long journey.

SONG 1: Emmanuel is born

SWEETIE: It wasn't so easy
It was a tough journey
Fourteen long years
for this child to be born

LUIS: There were moments we were fighting
Blaming…fingers pointing
And yet we knew
God was with us

SIMON: Yes, we too thought you were barren
and told you to abandon
the hope you had
that someday … this child would be born

ANNA: I just admire
the way you simply trusted

You both would not just give up
and so the Lord has given you Emmanuel…….

ALL: Emmanuel….Emmanuel
You are an answer
to all our silent prayers
Emmanuel….Emmanuel
You bring joy
to our patient hearts….

Scene 2

(Small Christian Community Prayer meeting at home)

NARRATOR: And the boy grows up. As he grows in age…he grows in mischief…He is 14 years of age now….and full of surprises.

SWEETIE: Emmanuel, our neighbours will come over to our place today for prayer. And I want you to behave yourself.

EMMANUEL: Mom….are the 20 packets of biryani you've ordered today meant to be given to all these uncles and aunties after prayer?

SWEETIE: Yes, son

EMMANUEL: Mom… simple biscuits…or boiled grams wouldn't do?....the way our old Pedrin does whenever we go to her house for prayer?

SWEETIE: She is poor…she can't afford….We are rich…so we must maintain our status.

EMMANUEL: Mom…What decides whether we are rich or poor? I find our old Pedrin…whom you called poor…so loving….so funny…she always makes me smile….So why are you rich and she poor?

SWEETIE: *(Furious)* Now….you've started again with your stupid questions. Just shut up and, as I told you, behave yourself with the guests.

(Enters Luis)

LUIS: Hey, Sweets…..Emmanuel….I'm back…on time for prayer…I saw some neighbours moving towards our place.

(A knock on the door) (Sweetie welcoming her neighbours - Anna, Simon, Catherine, Bruno - who are assembling at her place for the small Christian community meeting)

SWEETIE: Come in…. please find yourselves a chair and feel comfortable.

BRUNO: Hey Emmanuel….I thought you would be gone with your friends to play football.

EMMANUEL: I wanted to….But I wanted to know what you oldies are up to this time. *(Laughs)*

LUIS *(admonishingly):* Emmanuel….that's not the way you talk with your elders….say sorry!

EMMANUEL: I'm sorry, Uncle Bruno…I didn't mean to hurt you…It's just that I have a lot of questions in my head….

LUIS: Emmanuel…be quiet and sit there at the corner.

ANNA: Luis…don't be so hard on the little boy…Don't forget you prayed so hard for him.

SWEETIE: I know…but sometimes he is so crazy….he has questions to which we have no answers….he drives us mad!

(Emmanuel laughs loudly…and makes some funny actions)

LUIS: *(yells)* Emmanuel! *(Emmanuel quietly sits in one corner)*

SIMON: Let's begin with one carol:

(All sing the carol, 'O Come all ye faithful

SIMON: Today, let's reflect on a passage from the Gospel according to St Mathew, chapter 22, verses 34 - 40.

The Greatest Commandment

34 But when the Pharisees heard that he had silenced the Sadducees, they came together. 35 And one of them, a lawyer, asked him a question, to test him. 36 "Teacher, which is the great commandment in the law?" 37 And he said to him, "You shall love the Lord your God with all your heart, and with all your soul, and with all your mind. 38 This is the great and first commandment. 39 And a second is like it, You shall love your neighbour as yourself. 40 On these two commandments depend all the

law and the prophets."

CATHERINE: *(Prays aloud)*

SONG 2: Abba…help us be kind

Father…through Jesus,
You remind us
of the greatest commandments
You want us to follow
As your loving children,
We ought to worship you alone
We ought to love you and our neighbour
he way we want to be loved by you.
Abba Father…. help us to be kind
Abba Father….help us show compassion

EMMANUEL: Aunty Catherine….I've been hearing you praying this way several times…I like the tune of your prayer….but does God not listen to your prayer?

CATHERINE: Son…God does listen to my prayer….He listens to all our prayers.

EMMANUEL: Well, you prayed…asking God to help you be kind and to help you be compassionate…

CATHERINE: Yes, I did…and God does help me to be kind.

EMMANUEL: I'm sorry…if I have not understood it right….you certainly are kind to me…..But why have you sent old *Pai*….your husband's father to an old age home?

Can't he stay in his own house? I just thought you were unkind to him....and would you have done that even to your own father?

SWEETIE: Emmanuel, behave yourself!

EMMANUEL: That's the only thing you teach me, Mom....(mimics) to behave myself.... You elders really confuse me sometimes. You pray so well.... but nobody thinks of old Pedrin and old Joao. They live alone. Their children come home only for the summer holidays from Bombay. Do you visit them? Do you help them to buy fish and vegetables from the market?

LUIS: Emmanuel.... everyone is busy with a lot of work of their own....and anyway...Pedrin and Joao know how to manage themselves...

EMMANUEL: Daddy...how intelligent you elders are! When it comes to being kind towards the old and the lonely elders of our village, you say they manage themselves....Infact, they can't manage themselves. My friends Carlos, Manjula, and Chuchu.... Every morning, we take turns to visit them and ask them what they need...and we buy it for them.... sometimes they don't even have sufficient money to buy fish and medicine. That's the reason why, my dear Mom, I'm sometimes late to school.

(All are stunned)

EMMANUEL: And what about my friend Joe? He passed his XII standard exams in distinction...He wanted to be a doctor....but didn't have the needed money to seek admission. Why couldn't any one of you try to help him?

Was it because he was not your son?

LUIS: Emmanuel…I think you are talking a bit too much…. Just go inside.

EMMANUEL: I'm sorry if I've been rude. It's just that I'm wondering where God is…. when you pray *(goes in)*

SWEETIE: Please don't mind this little brat. He does this to us every day! Not a single day without his questions. And he just now slipped the rabbit out…saying he bunks classes to help that old stinking Pedrin and Joao….and look at how these oldies are spoiling our children.

(Luis and Sweetie help pass biryani packets)

SIMON: ….but you need to discipline your child….he is speaking a bit too much for his age.

LUIS: Yes, we will do our best. Thank you for coming over.

Scene 3

(Emmanuel hanging out with his friends - the so-called Drunkards - Smokies - Addicts)

NARRATOR: Emmanuel is a 24-year-old man now. He loves doing what others dare not. He does not drink…smokes not…pots not…and yet his buddies - Carlos, Nixon & Jude are freaking drunkards….addicts…the smoking junkies…..

SONG 3: We the Junkies

ALL: They call us the junkies
Drunkards…addicts …smokies
They advise their children
to avoid our bad company

BERNARD: This man over here
He changed our book cover
He gave us a purpose to live for
He changed our destiny

NIXON: Being in our freaking company
is not so good for you, buddy
You drink not & smoke not
But they call you too… a junkie.

JUDE: And remember, Manju
How much she loved you
Her parents thought
You were unacceptable
So you lost a proposal.

EMMANUEL: What does it matter, my friends
If I lose the world and its wealth
I enjoy good sleep and great health
coz' I haven't lost my soul
Because God is with us all……

EMMANUEL: Well, buddies… this evening we are meeting at Pedrin's place… for our Christmas get-together… and don't forget it's her 90th birthday. The other oldies must be brought.

CARLOS: I will bring Joao, while Jude will drive Basil and Lynette. Bernard is doing the decorations. Nixon and Manjula are baking cakes and cookies.

JUDE: Emmanuel….five years back when you came to us asking for help to help the lonely oldies of our village - Pedrin, Joao, Basil and Lynette to remain home rather than be lodged in the old age homes as wanted by their children who are either in Mumbai or abroad - we thought you were a crazy teenager because who could be asking help from drug addicts and drunkards and freaking junkies like us?

NIXON: And he replied, God wants it, and I asked him Emmanuel….but where is that freaking God…..If there were God, then we would not be in this freaking condition…we would have someone…or something to live for!

BERNARD: And you remember what you told us:
(Mimicking) Well, do you really want someone to live for and something to live for? God has sent me with both.
And you assigned me to take care of old Pedrin. You asked Carlos to take care of Basil…and similarly, Nixon would help Joao, and Jude would help Lynette. That changed our life, man! That was the best Christmas ever! Emmanuel, you

gave us a reason to live for!

(All rush and hug him)

EMMANUEL: Well, junkies…let's have a junky funky Christmas celebration with our oldies this evening.

For whatever little kindness we show to the least of our brethren…we do it unto Christ…and that's true Christmas….and when we do that with joy…. You don't have to ask me anymore, "Emmanuel - but where is God?"…. for you know Him now loud and clear!

(Enter…. Catherine and Bruno)

SONG 4: Emmanuel…but where is God?

LUIS & ***SWEETIE***: Emmanuel….Emmanuel….
Son, we never understood you.

SWEETIE: Your gift to us at Christmas
was a gift of Love & Truth

LUIS: Even as a child, you challenged us
to be sensitive and kind.

BRUNO: We are sorry for being rude.

CATHERINE: We thought, how can our daughter marry a dude?

BOTH: We were wrong…you have our consent to marry her!

BRUNO: Hey, Lucky man Emmanuel
God has restored you in abundance
You chose to listen to your heart
And God simply blessed your path

EMMANUEL: How easy it is to miss the God in me…O my parents
How easy it is to give up on me…as a difficult child
How easy it is to complain… condemn & criticize
How easy it is to miss in Emmanuel…God in human form.

God, however, is patient and kind
God waits to manifest in His Best Time
God unleashes His presence to those in need
God is among us, blessing humankind

OLDIES (Pedrin, Joao, Lynette & Basil)

You better not shout, and you better not cry
You better not be rude, and I'm telling you why
The oldies are now happy in town

These boys, you call them Junkies
You think they are good for nothing
Our own children leave us alone and lonely
But these junkies care for our needs.

Christmas is a time to be kind
God in human form…we've got to find
Baby Jesus will bless us with a sound mind

Emmanuel…Emmanuel
God is among us ….
But where are you, O God?
Emmanuel…Emmanuel
God is in all of us… waiting to be loved.
Let the God in you and me love everyone!

PLAY THREE

ARE YOU THERE?

LENTEN MUSICAL

The Characters

The first production of this play was staged at Pai Tiatrist Hall, Margao, during the Lenten season of 2018 on 13 April 2019, with the following Cast:

JESUS	Trevor Barreto
MOTHER MARY	Sharon Barreto
MARY MAGDALENE, LAWYER	Meviya Rebello
MARY DOCTOR 2	Daisy Fernandes
SALOME ARCHITECT	Patsmenia D'costa
JOHN, BUILDER	Alerio Sequeira
SIMON OF CYRENE	Senglung Mossang
JUDAS ISCARIOT	Russel Da Cruz
PETER, COMEDIAN BOSTEĂO	Ronaldo Martin Fernandes
ANDREW, POLICE INSPECTOR	Edsel S. Rodrigues
THOMAS, DOCTOR 1	Efrem Luis
COMEDIAN HAWALDAR	Debbie Pereira
VERONICA, COMEDIAN DEMELLO	Nelia Pereira
JOSEPH OF ARIMATHEA, MLA	Domingos Soares
GONSAL	Jayesh Raut
SARPANCH	George sfx
MINISTER	Leslie Noronha
PRIEST	Ralph D'Souza
ENGINEER	Ashwin Carlos Costa

LEPER, STUDENT	Ignatius Noronha
JAMES,	Roy Rodrigues
DUMB MAN	Seby Mendes
BUSINESSMAN	Melvyn Noronha
NARRATOR 1	Domnic Alvares sfx
NARRATOR 2	Trina Fernandes

Concept, Script, and Direction by **ALLAN TAVARES** SFX
Music Composition and Arrangement by **PETER CARDOSO** SFX
Show Management by **RONCY BRAGANZA** SFX
Produced by PILAR MUSIC ACADEMY - GOA PROVINCE, **SOCIETY OF PILAR**

The Troupe of 'Are you there.'

Prelude

NARRATOR 1: (*enters from the center....spot on him*) The death of a criminal is justified by many-a-law. The death of an innocent remains a mockery of the laws in the world.....and what if the so-called criminal...well judged to be so...and executed as prescribed by the law....what if that criminal was an innocent man...what if that criminal was the Son of God?

A movie clip, showing soldiers mocking Jesus – scenes of scourging, crowning with thorns, Way of the Cross, and crucifixion

[*The choir front stage sings*]

[SONG 01: NOMAN TUKA]

CHOIR: Noman tuka Judevanchea Raza
Noman tuka Judevanchea Raza

SOLO: Raza khoim to judevancho
Vo chor Nazaretcho
CHOIR: Sang re pixea tum Raza koslo
Podvi naslolo
Noman tuka Judevanchea Raza
Noman tuka Judevanchea Raza

NARRATOR 1: (*enters from the cross end towards the other narrator seated on a wayside boulder*) Were you there when they crucified my Lord? Were you there when they nailed Him to a tree?

NARRATOR2: It causes me to tremble...tremble...tremble....

[SONG 02: WERE YOU THERE?]

CHOIR: Were you there when they crucified my Lord? (2)
Oh, sometimes it causes me to tremble, tremble, tremble
Were you there when they crucified my Lord?

Were you there when they nailed him to a tree? (2)
Oh, sometimes it causes me to tremble, tremble, tremble
Were you there when they nailed him to a tree?

Scene one

A movie clip, showing darkness and tempest that covers the whole land...Music of tempest
The body of Jesus is seen in the lap of his mother, at the foot of the cross. Mary Magdalene, Mary the mother of James the younger and of Joses, Salome, and John the apostle, surrounds Mother Mary.... At one corner is seated Simon of Cyrene.
[*Peter walks back to Calvary*]

[SONG 03: Forgive me]

PETER: Oh, what a wretched creature I have been
He loved me, and I denied him
When he needed me the most, I ran away from the scene
Oh Lord, I have sinned. Forgive me. (2)

Forgive me, O Dear Mother
You are brave, though your heart is torn
Forgive us, O dear John
We ran away…You stood alone.

O come…O come…come back O my brothers.
Come back… come back home.
Let's honor the blood of our Savior.
Let us not be traitors anymore. (2)

PETER: (*yelling out*) We have not been there for the Lord when He needed us the most. Let us not be traitors anymore. O come…O come…come back O my brothers.

[*A few other apostles – Andrew, James & Thomas - who had run away, walk back to Calvary*]

[*All gather around Mother Mary and John, caressing the body of their Master*]
[*Choir sings the motet 'Dukhest Avoi'*]

[SONG 04: DUKHEST AVOI] (STABAT MATER)

***CHOIR*:**

1. Stabat mater dolorosa
   Juxta crucem lacrimosa – dumpende bat filiens
2. Dukhest avoi dukamborit
   Put umkolltalo tea vellim
   Ubi asli khursamullim

3. Stabat mater dolorosa
   Juxta crucem lacrimosa – dumpende bat filiens

***SALOME*:** (consoling her sister, Mary - mother of Jesus) You walked the last mile, O Brave one, knowing well that this son of yours was really not yours. You raised him to think of God as His Father...and lo...he was always busy with His Father's business. It was never about you, nor about him, nor about an innocent man being condemned to the death of a criminal. For you, it was always about being connected to God's story of our salvation. It was always about playing your part in this script of our redemption.

***JAMES*:** O Maim, ieta ugddas tuka tea disacho jednam tuvem amkam vele Somiashim ani sanglem taka mhaka ani mhojea bhavak Zuanvank diunk mukhel zago tachea rajeant?
Zuanvan sambal'lo to zago raun ubo Somiachea khursa mullim punn hanvem marli poll!

PETER: Hoi James ami chukle amchi vatt. Mhakai ugddas ieta koso hanvem patieun mhojeach bollacher marle bobke mhojea Somiak ani jednam vell ailo nakarlo taka sobhemazar.... nakarlo taka sobhemazar.....Ugddas ieta koso Somi polletalo to mhaka jednam tisrea pautt sad ghatlo tea kombean

(A movie clip, showing Jesus gazing at Simao after the latter denies him three times.)
[*Choir sings ' Jezu ani Simao'*]

[SONG 5: Jezu ani Simao]

CHOIR: Simao mhojea ixtta, kiteak tum bhieloi?
Kiteak tum lojeloi?...mhaka nakarloi?
Simao mhojea ixtta, tujer tum patieloi
Mhaka dubavloi…sodun mhaka geloi

Hanvem tuzo mog kela
Visvas tujer thevla
Tuka vhoddil nemla
Tuka bogxilla.

PETER: Hoi Dhonia…Hoi Dhonia...Tuka hanvem nakarloi
Bhielo hanv, lojelo hanv...Nakarlo hanvem mhojea Dhoniak
Punn soddun hanv tuka vechonam...Porgot'tolom hanv tujem nanv
Jem hanv korunk xokonk nam...Tachem farikponn ditolom hanv

A movie clip, showing people shouting "crucify him" "crucify him" before Pilate…as the choir sings the Motet: Formonn kiteak Jezucher?
[The apostles painfully recall these moments]

[Simon of Cyrene, who was sitting on a rock at a corner…rises and agitatedly questions the apostles]

[SONG 06: Formonn kiteak Jezucher?]

***SIMON OF CYRENE*:**

Formonn kiteak Jezucher?
Virod kiteak Jezucher?
Sotteo kiteak Jezucher?
Khuris kiteak Jezucher?

***CHOIR*:**

Formonn kiteak Jezucher?
Virod kiteak Jezucher?
Sotteo kiteak Jezucher?
Khuris kiteak Jezucher?

[Andrew walks up to Simon of Cyrene]

ANDREW:

Simao…. Simao… Simao
Xabaski tuka Simao
Baradik khuris gheun jednam chol'lo Somi.......

A movie clip shows Simon of Cyrene assisting Jesus on the way to Calvary.

[SONG 07: Xabaski tuka Simao]

ANDREW:

Simao…. Simao… Simao
Xabaski tuka Simao
Baradik khuris gheun jednam choltalo Somi.
To khuris ubarunk adarachi goroz asli
Ami bhieun pod kadli
Doiall kornni tuvem keli
Somiak adar tunvem dilo
Cholunk vat khursachi.

ANDREW: *(DIALOGUE)*

To khuris ubarunk adarachi goroz asli
Ami bhieun pod kadli
Doiall kornni tuvem keli
Somiak adar tunvem dilo
Cholunk vat khursachi.

[Peter rises]

PETER: Ugddas (2).... ieta ugddas....Jezuchea Nimmannea jevnnacho (Jn13/2 - 17) *(A movie clip shows Jesus' interaction with Peter at the last supper)*

[SONG 08: UGDDAS IETA]

Ugddas ieta mhaka Nimmannea jevnnacho
Penkttak bandun tuvalo,
Somi paiem dhuunk laglo.
Hem koslem kortutv mhojea Somiachem,
tem somzunk mhaka avgodd zalem

PETER: Koslem mhonn kortutv hem mhojea

Somiachem......Somia tum mhoje paim dhutai........
[choir sings the motet: Dhonia tum mhoje paim dhutat?]

[SONG 9: Dhonia tum mhoje paim dhutai?]

CHOIR:

Dhonia tum mhoje paim dhutai?
Jem kam hanv kortam, tem tum somzochonai
Uprant somzotoloi
Ah mhojea Dhonia
Mhoje paim dhuvunk hanv diunchonam tuka

JAMES: Nimannea jeunnar Jezun dovorli nixanni aplea sasnnik mogachi. Keli tust tannem vinomr seve-chakrechi. Nimannem jevonn kortokoch, vatt dhorli Somian Gethsemani molleachi

(A movie clip shows Jesus in the garden of Gethsemane.)

[SONG 10: Gelo Somi magnnem korunk]

JAMES: Nimannem jevonn kortokoch,
Gelo Somi Gethsemani molleant
Ugddas kelo soglleank amkam
magnnem korunk…chottur raunk (2)

JAMES: Ugddas kelo soglleank amkam magnnem korunk…chottur raunk (2)

LEPER: *(dashes into the scene, shouting)* Hey, where is Jesus? (sees his limp body in the bosom of Jesus' Mother and falls prostrate before them) Why do we kill those who do good?

NARRATOR 2: *(walks towards him)* Who are you? Who is Jesus to you?

LEPER: I am that leper from Samaria... He cured me on his way to Jerusalem....I didn't know they would do this to him.....I reached late...I could have stopped them from this act of cold-blooded murder! (turning to the apostles) Tumi khoi gel'le re? Marunk dilo re tumi taka?

[The choir sings the motet: Riglo Jezu]

[SONG 11: Riglo Jezu]

Choir:

Riglo Suam Jezu molleant
Dhian ani orasanvant
Diuncheak Farikponn Purthem
Adanvanchea rinnanchem

JOHN: Pedruk, mhaka ani Jamesak gheun gelo Somi tea Gethsamanichea bhagint. Amkam tannem sanglem: 'Tumi hanga bosat ani magnnem korat". Somi anink fuddem gelo ani poddlo aplea dimbiencher ani vhoddlea tallean aplea Bapa lagim uloilo: 'Bapa...atam mhojea jivacher akant aila...hanvem kitem mhonnchem? Bapa, hea vellantlo mhaka nivar oxem mhonnum? Na, heach pasot hanv hea vellak pavlam. Bapa tujea nanvak mhoima zoddun ghe."
Ani ami nidechea bhorman poddle. Ek tas-bhor Somiachea borobor zage ravunk amchean nozo zalem. *(...and John breaks down...while Peter comes over to him)*

PETER: "Zagrut ravat ani magnnem korat" Ho ugddas tannem amkam kelo

[choir sings the motet: Gethsamani molleant]

[SONG 12: Gethsemani molleant] cf: Lk 22/39 *(choir 8)*

CHOIR:

Gethsemani molleant magnnem kortana
Rogot humelo amchea pasun…amchea pasun

Patkacho bhar tujea mathear gheun
Xisank polleunk gelo, nidleat kai mhonn
Xinn tuvem keloi (3) tujea xisam lagim

Ekuch hor tumcheamnim, magnneamnim sarunk zaunk nam (2)
Mhoje pasot, tumche pasot, porje pasot

LEPER: Punn kainch korunk zaunk nam tumcheamnim addaunk hi dharun kornni?

PETER: Jednam Jezuk vorunk te aile....hanvem proitn kelo addaunk. Mhoji torsad kadun hanvem katorlo tea mha-iadnikachea sirvidoracho...malcusacho kan. Punn anink fuddem kitem-i korunk (pointing to Jesus) tannem adailo mhaka....(goes to Jesus)....anink hanvui bhielom.....

ANDREW: Sandun gele Somiak ami soglle dadle. Bailamnim sangat dilo gorjechea vellar. Magdalachi Maria, Juanv ani Jamesachi avoi - Salomi, Joses ani dakttea Jamesachi avoi, Maria . *[Veronica enters with the towel with which she had wiped the face of Jesus]* ani Veronica chol'lim Somiachea Avoichea sangata ti baradik khursachi vatt ani dakoili niz kallji....hannim dakoili amkam niz kallji.

[SONG 13: Mhojea Jezu]

VERONICA (*backed by choir*):

Mhojea Jezu…Mhojea Jezu
Rumalar tuzo rupkar pollelo
Hanvem pollelo (3)
Sobitai nam, suropai nam
Koslich taka sundorai nam
Konn tachi porva korinam…porva kori nam.

MARY MAGDALENE: Death cannot put to rest a legacy of life Divine.....Death cannot steal away a noble man...Death cannot for sure silence a life of compassion.....In this world of men, for whom a woman is just a woman....and just a possession....in such a world, lived this man who understood and dignified my vocation as a woman. He shared with us His vision. He dared to allow us to walk by his side on His mission.

THOMAS: You are so right, O Mary. We men only boasted about what we thought we could....but when the moment arrived...we just ran....away from purpose and destination. You showed guts, O women. How uncomfortable I felt to have you in our company, especially in Galilee. Pardon me, O Mary, for the doubts I carried. You triumphed with your unflinching faith, while I remained merely doubting!

[SONG 14: He is my Lord]

***MARY MAGDALENE*:**

He is my Saviour…He is my Lord
He doubted not and caressed my soul
He lifted me from sinful hell
Restored me to heavenly health.

They distorted his face and crucified him
Yet from the cross, He forgave them
Lo behold…His limp body in the arms of His mother
And yet I know/He is risen to the bosom of His Father

He is my Saviour…He is my Lord
He doubted not and caressed my soul
He lifted me from sinful hell
Restored me to heavenly health.

[As Mary Magdalene sings, Joseph of Arimathea & other women come in with incense and perfume. They anoint the body of Jesus and wrap it to be taken to the tomb.]

Scene Two

The Mount of Calvary with the cross of Jesus. Sound of wind blowing across. [choir sings "The old rugged cross" as some contemporary Christians contemplate on the Calvary scene....the 'Dumb' man is kneeling at the foot of the cross. One elderly blind man sitting on a rock]

NARRATOR 1: On a hill far away...stood an old rugged cross...the emblem of suffering and shame....and I love that old rugged cross

[SONG 15: The old Rugged Cross]

***CHOIR*:**

On a hill far away
Stood an old rugged cross
The emblem of suffering and shame
And I love that old rugged cross
Where the dearest and best
For a world of lost sinners was slain

So I'll cherish the old rugged cross
Till my trophies at last I lay down
I will cling to the old rugged cross
And exchange it someday for a crown

Oh, that old rugged cross
So despised by the world
Has a wondrous attraction for me
For the dear lamb of God
Left His glory above
To bear it toward Calvary.

NARRATOR 2: On this holy wood, Jesus died and rose to eternity. I remember what that leper asked: Why do we kill those who do good? Hi Kotha Jezuchi...Hi Kotha Jezu sarke borem kortolea monxamchi? Krist mhonn ami Jezuk pachartanv...Buddha mhonn ami Gautamak ollkotanv...Mahatma mhonn ami Gandhik vakanttanv. Krist, Buddha, Mahatma...nhoi alkunj tanchi...Jesus was declared as Christ for He truly lived as the Beloved Son of God. Jezuk ami Christ mhonn man ditanv kiteak tannem niz sotan ani mogan jieun Devachem ek vishesh Rup amkam ollkunk dilem.

DUMB MAN: (shouts at the Narrator) Puro kor tujem uloup! Hoi Jezu khorench Krist koso jielo punn goroz nasli taka khursar marunk? We don't have to kill good people to prove their goodness! We need to change our wicked ways and allow the good people to live and inspire us!

NARRATOR: Tum mono ulounk laglo?

DUMB MAN: Hoi! Devan aple kalutin mhoji jib portun sudov kelea! *(The dumb man is stunned that he spoke!)* Tuka godiek khobor aschinam ki hanv mono koso zolmunk nam. *(recalls and narrates about his past)* Mumboiche courtint mhaka govai koso ubo kel'lo sot tem sangunk, punn poixeanche axen ani....bhirantin....hanvem fott marli anink eka niropradi monxachea crimidorak suttka favo keli....Devan mhaka khast laili. Eka mhoinean mhoji jibb zodd zaun mhojem uloup bond zalem....vis vorsam sarlim ek mono koso. Gel'lim Dha vorsam niz pirachit hanvem kelem....Devaxim hanv portolom...ani mhoji jib....sotak govai diunk aiz Devan sodoili!

NARRATOR: So you think you will now stand for truth? Sota pasot tum zuzhtolo atam?

DUMB MAN: Goroz tednanch....utramnim nhoim...magnnean

ani pirajitan uloitolom hanv

[Minister, Local MLA, Sarpanch, Priest, along with bouncers, enter watching the Calvary scene]
[Projected on Screen....the batim hill, the royal road, and the Batim lake]

MINISTER: Matse rav, Khursaxim vathi pettoun ietam?
GONSAL (ELDERLY VILLAGER): Vath kiteak pettoitat Sir? Konnachench objection nastanam urlolo dongorui kobar korun uddounk? Ho dongrar axil'lo khuris, tumim haddun zomnir bosoila. Hea dongrachea khursa mullim altar bandun amcho St Francis Xavier ani St Jose Vaz mis kortale...Hea dongravoilean te ani sabhar missionar cholun Vhoddlea Goiam vetale.....Hea dongra veleo zorio, khuxik aslelea tolleank, xitoll udkan bortaleo ani hea tolleant voros bhor amkam rosroshit nistem melltalem ani sonvsarachim veg-vegllim suknnim udun hangam ietalim.
MLA: Gonsal, Siracho vell pidear korinaka...ami magir ulounchem
GONSAL: Vell ani uronk nam Sir, amchem ghotton zaupachem niktench asa!

[SONG 16: Politicians and Villagers at Calvary]

GONSAL: Kiteak tumim ho dongor kapunk dilo?
Hi girestkai ogdaun koslo dudu zoma kelo?
Rosteachea nanvan luttunk tuka Dencharan nadlo?
Dhadoxi jieunche bodlek lenvtto tuka kelo!

MLA: Thoddio vostu tumim somzochenant?
"Haka lutt ani taka di" hem ami-i anvddenant
Poixeam vinnem gorzank pavonk ami xokonant!

Chodd sotan jielear elesanvam ami jikchenant

DUMB MAN: Oxem uloun Devan dil'le gunnachi ninda korinaka
Devan porjecho fuddari zaunk soeg tumka dila
Ho karbhar cholounk Devuch bolaiki dita
Dil'le sotiecho faido kaddunk denchar tuk' buloita.

MLA: (shouts) Hoi....chodd uloup zata tumchem....

MINISTER: (yells back at the MLA) Te kainch chodd ulounk nant. Khorem mhonnlear tannim mhaka khursar marunk zai aslo. Bolteankuch khursar martat! Jednam osle ontoskornn aslele monis sot amchea tonddar martat tednam amchi podvi...dudu uzar korun ami tankam nanch kortat....oxem korun ami ghodiek somzotat, ami amchi vatt saf keli mhonnun.....fotoitat ami amkanch.

Hanv khursaxim ailam, bogsonnem magunk. MLA Bab, tuvem hea rosteacho udorgitichea tujea illakean choltolea kamacho boro faido kaddunk ievjilem...mhaka phone marlo....mhojem boremponn ghetlem...mhojem mhaka meulem....Sarpanch Bab tuven ek avaz voir kaddunk nam...tuvem virodd korunk nam...lokachem mot geunk nam...tum bhielo....ani oxem korun Ho dongor...Hi adleamnim samballe'li dhormik ani srishttik sonskrutai ami apsvarthi axen ani lenvtteponnan nanch keli....Hanv somzolom mhojea hikmotin ani mhojea bollan hanvem mhaka zai tem korunk zata. zaite bore monis mhaka addaunk sodthale tanchi beporva hanvem keli...

PRIEST: Bhava mhojea.....amchi-i ti chuk! Ami tumche dhormik fuddari. Ami tumchem marg dorxonn korunk zai. Ami tumche fottkire amig vortoule... sot kitem tem sangche bodlek ami tumkam fokot mosko lailo...Fotti budh tumkam dili....tumchem boremponn samballunk ami tumchem canvassing pasun kelem. Kednam pasun hem dongi jivit ami jieteleanv

MINISTER: Are dongeamnom.....naka mhaka tumchi ixttagot! I don't want your friendship or your justification. I just want God's mercy. I am at the cross today to tell the Lord that I have faulted....and if I am given a chance...I would, like St Paul, turn it all around! I mean it, Lord *(falls on his knees)*

Hea khorezmant, hanv mhojem jivit bodoltam......

Politik nhoi khursecho faido kaddun porjek naddunk ani dovlot komaunk....Politik soeg Devachem mogachem ani nitichem raj hea sonsarant ami sthapit korunk.

COMEDIAN BOSTEANV: Avois....hing kit cholot re.....inspectiona eileaii kit re! Sarpanch, MLA ani Ministerui eil mure....Fatherui asa mure..ganvch lokui asa....Gram Sabha cholota kitem? khursa vatt kotaie kite re?

PRIEST: Bosteanv...voi...amchem patok ami roddtanv...hea Calvarichea khursa mullim.

[SONG 17: Politicians & Priests at Calvary]

PRIEST

Khursachi vatt ami choltanv
Amche dongi jivit nakartanv
Jezuche mornacher nialltanv
Jivit bodlunk tachi kurpa magtanv

MINISTER:

Tujea khursa sorlo pois hanv gelam Somia
Fottingponnan hanv jielam Dhonia
Sot uloiteleank hanvem sasnak oge kele
Jivit bodlunk hanv Sodtam Saiba

COMEDIAN DEMELO: Avois....Minister Saiba...tuj bhaxen

jivit bodlop mhollear kitem re! Hairstyle change koropu?....Bank account change koropu?.....Car change koropu?

DUMB MAN: Demelo....fokannam kornaka....goddiek Sir khoreamninch anvddeta ek borem jivit!

COMEDIAN DEMELO: Are monea tum pis zala.....Henk eso nattkam korpa sonvoi! Atam elesanv bogle paulo naim - i? elesanvam poile exech kongre zan einai tem amge ghara?....tedonn khorem amge mogan baztai exe disnai he?....elesanv zalem...marlo hujov....hanv ani tum amge hompinkum urle....enge bongle...enge motram...enge poixe...vaddot gele....Sir....pikar zainakanv.....tum matse bore moodan asa mhonn pottantum soglem uloitam....pottam chodd temp rag dovorpa xiri ponnam!....num re Father....ell deunch poilo rag bhair udoupa zaio!

MLA: Borem...zori tor hanv-ui khoreanich mhojem jivit bodlunk sodtam zalear tumi mhaka koxe bhaxen adhar diunk xoktole?

PRIEST: Ami fuddari lokache. Jezuchea kallar, Iadnik, Dhormi xastri, Pilat ani Herod raza asle fudari lokache. Tanche modem jednam Jezu upzolo ek niz lokachea mogacho fuddari koso tednam Iadnikamnim ani Dhormi xastreamnim taka svikarunk nam. Nattkai tankam zali... Pilat ani Herod, Jezuchem moluch somzonk nant. Jezuk marunk te soglle bhagi zale!!!

[choir sings the motet "ladnik ani Dhormxastri" as characters of the stage try to grapple with their issues in mute]

A movie clip shows Pharisees plotting against Jesus

[SONG 18: IADNIK ANI DHORMXASTRI]

CHOIR:

Sonsot ami…sonsot Abramachi
Devachea mogachi
Magnnem korpi…upas korpi
Somurtik visvaxi

Magnnem ami kortanv
Somurt pallunk laitanv
Huxarkai hi amchi
Dekhun Jezuk fudden koria…korum-ia choukoxi

Nazaretkar ho lokak bhuloita
Taka ami dhorum-ai
Ochoriam korun amkam lojek ghalta
Taka dhorun bandhum-ia

Deva put mhonn soglleank sangta
Formonn marum-ia
Khuris diun lojek galum-ia
Tacher taka khillaum-ia

NARRATOR 2: Advogad bai, tum sang mhaka...hantunt chuk konnachi? borem kortelea Jezuchi? vo lojek poddlolea nitidarachi?

ADVOGAD: Zaite pautt, sot uloilear nit zaina

NARRATOR 2: Punn sot poisailear, nit khoinchi?

ADVOGAD: Case jikop hem odhik gorjenchem. Sot samballunk, poixeancho nett lagta....ani poixeanchi beporva kelear, amchem pott konn bhortolo?

NARRATOR 1: Poixeanchea forsan case jikon niropradeak

khursar marun koslem dhadossponn tuka?

[Sound of Police siren...Police officers enter]

POLICE OFFICER: Sir, tumkam konnem tras kele?

MINISTER: Punn, tumkam konnem hanga apoileat?

COMEDIAN HAVALDAR: Nam Sir...matse confuzanv zalem! Konnem eklean phone malo....morcha kaddli mhonn katorlo dongrakodde.... ani konnem phone marlo aiz khursa vatt kotai mhonn katorlo dongra kuxi kursa kodde....ani konnem phone marlo Minister Saib, MLA Saib ani Sarpanch Saib rodttai mhonn katorlo dongra kuxi tollea kodde....All events happening at katorlo dongra kodde....dangerus...Tek lagon Siren on korn ami eileai Sir!

MINISTER: Inspector Bab, Lawyer Bai....hanv mhojem jivit bodlunk anvddetam....(*to inspector*) Zaite pautt hanvem tuka phone marun pressure ghatlam borea monxank tras diupak ani mhojea monxank vattaupak...*(to lawyer)* Tukai-i hanvem domki dileat case mhaka zai te bhaxen ghunvddaupak. Kednam pasun osleach bollan hanv jietolom....Tumi-i mhaka xirap bi ghatlea astele nhoi?

POLICE: Sir! Dev tumkam axirvadan borum...jem tum anvddeta tem goddon ieum...Police ami lokache rakhondar! Ani zori tor tumi amche fuddari sotan ani nitin jiele.....zalear ami-i lokacho bhavarth amcher vaddounk pautele....nam zalear zaite pautt tumchea forcan amchea ontoskornant borem disonam tem pasun ami kortanv....Amchem-i jivit ami bodlunk zai!

SARPANCH: Hanv chintalo....kiteak mhonnon hanv MLA-chea ani Ministeranchea bhirantin, tanchea palveant jietam.....fotingponnan kiteak mhonnun hanv naka tim licensam ditam....Oslea bhirantin vo naddbudhin mhoji bolaiki hanvem ogdaili....diabetes...pressure...vaddot veta. Khorem mhonnlear mhozo ganvcho lok - mhoji khori takot!....mhojea ganvchi sonskrutai - mhoji khori girestkai!....kitlo sontos ani dhaddosponn mhaka bogunk zai mhojea ganvchi hi girestkai rakhunk ani mhojea ganvcheank feliz korunk!

COMEDIAN BOSTEANV: *(to comedian Demelo)* Hench aik....ami amge sarpanchink, Ministarank, Adogaddank, policink, choru monnpa urle......Choi kit korn te soglle bore monis zaupa sodtai te!

COMEDIAN DEMELO: Tuge mistek went wrong! Correction korpa poddtolem.. adogadan mhonlam borem zaupa sodit mhonnum?....*(to lawyer)* mhonlam go tuem? *(she moves towards the cross)* Sorry anv....I no get your signal! ani padrim galunk naim mure tuem te choram listanku? Todde Padri horench Deva monis....thodde padri amkam lokak fotoitai...chortai....

DUMB MAN: Bhavamno...ho vell bexttoch eka-mekachea dolleantlim kuskuttam kaddun ami ibadd korcho nhoim! Ho vell jivitachea novsornnecho!

COMEDIAN BOSTEANV: Hanv tench mhonnpa sodtalom....ami dusream chor...lofor...fotting, mhonnpa sompem....Demelo...poir ami xezreage dukor chorlo nam? Bosam lokange pakitt mahnaim ami? Nixttea inktastonam...pomxelom nixtea mistur kornaim ami?.....anim sangpa zaiem?.....ami mhonn bore?....bexttech dusreanku bottam dakoix num...Amge dolleantu hollim poilim bhair kaddea!

COMEDIAN DEMELO: Are Bosteanv...tuem amge chorie record samki declare keli mure....

[SONG 19: JIVIT BODLOP DENNEM KURPECHEM]

NARRATOR 2:

Jivit bodlop kam Devachem
Jivit bodlop dennem kurpechem
Niz kallzacheank mellta tem
Nam boreponn Deva kurpe vinnem

POLICE:

Eka mekak sangat ami dium-ia
Vaittovem jivit nopoit korum-ia
Fottingponn unttaun kaddum-ia
Borem kortoleank tenko dium-ia

BUILDER: Sir, ami site - ir rautat tumkam...tumi khursa-xim vetat te ami pollele...ami somzole tumi magnnem korun rokddech ietele mhonnun....punn boro vell tumi khursaxi kaddlo...Is everything OK Sir....He Ganv ke admi kuch lafda to nahim kar rahe hai nam?

MLA: Dilip....Jyada mat bol...Sir mood me nahim hai....

MINISTER: Nahim to.... hum aj perfect mood me hain! Baba Dilip....ho dongor tuvem katorla to puro...tujem kam aiz sun bondh....We don't need more mud from here for the road....infact it was not about the road at all!

ARCHITECT: Yes, that's the point...It was not about mud for the road...it was more about clearing this hill for our project!.. Our MLA had called us today to make a Master Plan. This meeting between all of us was to brainstorm at the site and initiate a blueprint for all the possible options....factory or residential block.....and also about our shares...and....

ENGINEER: So....now... does this project...and this plan...stand cancelled?

MLA: Hoi sodheak cancel!

COMEDIAN DEMELO: Sodhea, cancel monnllea kit re Sir? Elesanva toiari?

SARPANCH: Demello, jitle ami nadd title ami Devache kurpen bore-i zaunk xoktanv

MLA: Mhojea pasot mag Demello....tum chinta toshem hanvem korina zaunk...Fattim hanvem toxench kelam....elesanvam jikpak lokak mhojem borem rup dakoilam..vo poixeanchi axa hanvem porjek dilea....hanv toshem fuddarak korunk anvddena...punn tumchea magnneanchi ani Devache Kaklutichi bik hanv hea vellar magtam.

[SONG 20: Builders at Calvary]

BUILDER:

I think as a builder, I was a bulldozer
I had money...so bought off people's fields and hills in a whiffer
Lokachim battam chorunk mhaka kainch num zalam...
Amcho ganvcho lok samko nennar....
kitleach zannank hanvem fottoileant....
Vhoddlea xovtteanche Cruttanim gheop...ani amchea ganvchea lokank biknnam vanttop....hi mhoji kala....
Permissions and licenses were never a problem
I got them all…**<u>it was all about money</u>**

ARCHITECT:

I want to seek pardon
An architect....that's what I am
I designed in haste and caused great risk
Thought the faster the better…

Devan boreo imaroteo ani ghoram rochun haddpachem xikop mhaka favo kelam
Hi Devachi zannvai uzar korun hanvem udorgotik ek novench rup diunk xoktalem....punn fatta fatt drawings korun kaddun hanvem zaite poixe keleat.....
Yes it was all about money

ENGINEER:

And even if it was a good design that you gave me
I just gave it to contractors who can please me
An engineer....that's me... playing with people's safety
Pardon me Lord... **it was all about money**

DUMB MAN: Hea khursacher nodor poddtanch....Rogot xizta mhojea xirant.
Niropradi tornatteak nattak kelo eka apsvarthi dharun kortutvan
Farizev, dhormxastri lokache dhormik fuddari zale Jezuche dusman
Herod ani Pilat Politisian. Salvar korunk zatalo Jezuk...punn
Apleponnan dilem mornachem formonn.

GONSAL: Tumi jem hea kursa mullint uloileat tem kortutvant ghalat bhurgeamno. Minister Bab, MLA Bab, Sarpanch Bab tumchea porjecho niz mog korat. Lokachea kallzamnim tumchem ghor bandat. Elesanvamchea vellar motam chorunk Denvchar nadtolo. Tumi ek retir korat....ani Otmeanchea ogeponnan Devachi omollik zannvai tumkam melltoli....te zannvaie pormonnem cholat.

[Narrator 2 observes the doctors and interacts with them]

NARRATOR 2: Hey, Doctors, what brings you here to this old rugged cross?

DOCTOR 1: Oh, some patients told us that there is a retreat going on here at the cross! I've been reflecting on my savior...and I think I, too, am lost.

DOCTOR 2: God has bestowed on us the gift of saving lives. But some like me are only improving our business styles. Dev aplea dotoram udexim monxank aplem jivit ani pekovnni diunk anvddeta punn hanv fokot mhojem business vaddounk axetam.

DOCTOR 1: So often have I simply made the patients linger in my hospital.

DOCTOR 2: My patients trust me like God, and I treat them like vegetables. Khorench...mhojea patientank hanv Dev...punn mhaka sogllech patient ek sarke....jitle odik patient titlech odik poixe zoddop.

[A student enters]

STUDENT: (aside) That's Mr. Crusoe, my Professor! (to professor) Hello Professor...good to see you here...What do you say of so many innocents dying on the altar of Capitalism, Nationalism, and Communalism?

PROFESSOR: Oh ....you do know to ask intelligent questions... I always thought of you as dumbo in my class!

STUDENT: Professor...do you at least know that I am a third-year undergraduate student...or do you still think I am a first-year student?

PROFESSOR: Oh ...are you already a third year?

STUDENT: Professor...if I am not mistaken...as a very senior faculty.....especially with the seventh pay commission so gracious towards you...you are earning more than a lakh of Rupees per month...Do you really give back in the same proportion to the college and to us, your students!

PROFESSOR: I think you are going a little arrogant.

STUDENT: Professor...I'm sorry if I sounded rude...I just wanted to know...are you, as my professor, really passionate about transforming me into a responsible leader and a breadwinner? Are you?

PROFESSOR: I think I have completed my portion. I do take all my classes...usually!

STUDENT: Professor...I'm sorry if I sound rude again...Do you think you are paid so much for so little....just presenting the same lecture you've been delivering for donkey years...passing around those dusty notes which we are supposed to swallow for exams...picking some old dissertations for projects year after year.

PROFESSOR: I hope you know we also have a family to cater to. Besides being your teacher, I also have responsibilities as a Father and a husband...

STUDENT: Professor...No doubt we see very little of you, besides your class hours...and you disappear at
1 o'clock.....

PROFESSOR: Why are you racking up all this nuisance!

STUDENT: Professor... I, as a simple student of a Christian institution, expect more of you. How are you different, then, as a Christian? Can't I expect a different set of Christ-like values from you?.... Do you empower me to transform my neighborhood?

PROFESSOR: Are you trying to tell me that I am selfish? (Aside) Perhaps.... he is right!

[SONG 21: Jesus destroyed sin]

NARRATOR 2:

Devachim bhurgim ami sogllim
Ami zaunk xokonant gulam axechim
Sonvsarant gazounk zai Devachi mhoima ami
Devachi bhurgim monxam kurpechim

NARRATOR 1:

The mortal sin of doubting Divine Providence
made us humans - slaves of endless desire
Jesus' sacrifice on that rugged cross
destroyed sin and death in eternal fire

NARRATOR 2:

Could at least Christians
like Christ lay down their lives
And serve people with compassion?
Could they combine and serve the nation?

STUDENT: It's so good to see all of you together here at the foot of the cross. As youngsters, we really want to look up to you with respect and admiration. As politicians, you inspire us to hand over a safer planet and a civilized Society to the next generation. As lawyers and police officers, you make us feel protected and secure in our rights as citizens. You, our Professors and Priests, help rekindle the gift of the Divine within us. *(All move towards the student)* Doctors, Builders, Architects, Engineers....your original research and practice make us students aspire for true professionalism....and as professionals we ensure the livability of our Mother Earth and joyful living for each of us.

Yes! You are our heroes...Please make us by your lives feel proud of you.

MINISTER: Amchi Bhas ami tuka ditanv tornattea! Jezu bhaxen ami-i vavurtole pavounk Devachem boreponn sobhemazar. Jezun keli mogachi seva morun khursar.

COMEDIAN BOSTEANV: Shi Bhurgea kit uloil re tum......solid!...amge kaim mellonam tuka sangonku...tum matse late pavolo....tum ieche poilench haniem...

COMEDIAN DEMELLO: Oi Ogo Bosteanv...portun sangoxi amge sogllem.....

COMEDIAN HAVALDAR: Punn kalliz mon saf aslear kitu kuxal kai bogota num...Ani khorem ami uloileai te bhaxen zori kelem zalearu...jerul...ache din aienge!

[SONG 22: Don't crucify Truth]

NARRATOR 2:

Using our power to subdue truth
Is what crucified the Lord
Jealousy, hatred, and mere doubts
Made our Lord hang on that Cross

NARRATOR 1:

Adanv ani Eve dubhavlim Devachea boreponnacher
ani gelim add Devachea ievzonnecher
Ami...jednam dubhavtat ekamekacher
vetat ami add Devachea kakluticher

[play of Strobe lights... as the music and the mood change. All turn their attention to Judas Iscariot, who restlessly enters the scene]

[SONG 23: Judas Iscariot]

ALL ON STAGE:

Judas Iscariot…kitem tunvem kelem
Tea tis nanneank lagon…Devachem dennem ogddailem
Judas…Judas…Judas (2)

CHOIR:

Judas Iscariot…kitem tunvem kelem
Tea tis nanneank lagon…Devachem dennem ogddailem
Judas…Judas…Judas (2)

JUDAS:

Dolldiro hanv kitlo, Somiak hanvem viklo
Nimannea velar pasun, Mogan tannem mhaka lekhlo

CHOIR:

Tujem Patok rodd re Judas
Kor Jezuchea utrancho ugddas
Tujea patkak lagun to mela...Tujem patok pun to bhogxita

JUDAS:

Nam…Nam…Nam
Koslea tondan bhogsonnem magum hanv
Poixeanche axek lagun
Mhojea somiak hanvem khursar choddoila
Jiv mhozo hanv ditolom. Jivak mhojea valor nam

ALL ON STAGE:

Naka…Naka…Judas oxem korum naka
Jezu tuka bhogxita…aplo apostl Tannem tuka nemla
Tujea jivak valor asa mhonnuch to mela
Naka Judas…tuzo jiv ogddainaka

[Judas cries aloud out of frustration…breaks free from everyone and runs away in disgust with his life]
A movie clip shows Judas hanging himself from a tree

NARRATOR 1: Judas....O Judas...You could have forgiven yourself when the one whom you betrayed never counted you as bad! He forgave you as well!

MLA: Jezun taka kednanch poisanvunk nam

SARPANCH: Punn tachea konsiesan taka suseg diunk nam. Apsvarthi axecho jednam monis zata ghulam....ogddaita aplo otmo ani sorgacho inam.

ENGINEER: What does it profit me if I gain the world and lose my soul?

Architect: But how could Judas doubt his Master's goodness?

[Minister cries aloud out of frustration)

MINISTER: No.....it's not about Judas alone.....it's about me....it's about you.......we just don't want to change! We don't mind rotting in sin! Patkachi sonvoi zal'lea mhaka!

LAWYER: But I thought you were one of the most successful men around. Tum itlo vhodd Minister mhonntokoch tuvem kuxal asunk zai!

MINISTER: Voi! oxench chint tum mhojem! keep thinking good about me....and I am intelligent enough to make you think well about me. Jesus, at even a tender age of twelve, was busy doing his Father's business...that's what he told them when they came searching for him in Jerusalem.

He died on that wretched cross...again doing his Father's business of salvation....

and me as a Christian Minister...I am only busy making more money...I don't mind cheating...I don't mind bribing...I just want to think that I need more money....led by this greed....I continue to deny Him...I continue to betray him...again and again.... I am not there the way I could have been for the Lord...Nagoun...luttun fottoun poixe korpachi sonvoi zalea mhaka.....Jezucho xis kos hanv jiunk nam....jivachi ubgonn ailea mhaka....I don't deserve to live either....

LAWYER: My brother....You deserve to live....because He told us...."The thief comes only to steal and kill and destroy; I have come that they may have life, and have it to the full". Yes....as a Christian, I cannot live like a thief! As we get back to Calvary...let's resolve that we will steal no more...kill no more...destroy no more.... we shall live and let others live to the fullest! Jezu mela tuje pasot ani mhoje pasot, amchea jivitachem nisontonn korunk nhoi!...To mela amchem jivit dhadoxi korunk!

DOCTOR 1: Jesus did not sentence him to death...Jesus does not sentence us to death...I think He continues to say: "Father, forgive them....for they know not what they do!" Jesus died that we may value our lives.

COMEDIAN BOSTEANV: Sir, Amge Dev Doiall...mogall....tek naka tum melolo...tek zaio tum portun ek bor munis zalolo....fokot rebank portun voson ghotnaka...tum amge fuddari...tum zori sotan jielo... ami lok dhadoxi astole...ani ami zori dhadoxi zalear ami tuka ani girest kortolei...tuka, chorn...fotton girest zaupa goroz na... ami-i bhi lokamnim, sotan jiepa zaiem....ami-i amch ministarank poixeam ATM mhonn somzotai....ami tenkam sotan jieupa tank diupa zai-i...ani elesanvam vellar niz fuddareank soeg diupa zaio loka seva korpak....mot mat tem amchea faidea num....desa faideak...somestam faideak....borponn adpak, mot marpa zaiem.....

COMEDIAN BOSTEANV: Sir....mhaka bogos....haiem tujim

zaitim fokann kelim...punn tuj bhitor zaitem borem-i asa....vaitt asa tem sonn dhi.....borem asa tem vaddoi....Devan tuka fuddari zaupa dennem dilam....tuj jivita mol asa...tem maxe isronaka.....

[SONG 24: Jivit amchem molachem]

CHOIR:

Jivit amchem molachem
Devachench tem dennem
Apurbhaien jivit jiunk
Jezunuch amkam dakhoilem

Khursar tachem jivit somponk nam
Kuddicho jiv kaddlo zait pun otmo moronk nam
Borem jivit marun uddounk, mornak tank nam

Ulo amchea soddvonnaracho
Aiz kanar gheum-ia
Dubhav apsvartponn soddun
Mogan jieum-ia

PROFESSOR: (to narrator 1) Francis! You made me think! How easy it is to be selfish! How exciting it looks to be greedy! How angry I felt when you, as my student, hurt my pride! How clever I am in guarding my forts of selfishness...pride...and greed! And in all this, how foolish I become in losing what God bestows on me! How easily I dirty those precious pearls of TRUST...JOY....and PEACE....

STUDENT (FRANCIS): My dear Professor...I didn't mean to hurt you....it's just that we need you elders to be our role models....We want you to inspire us.

MINISTER: Voi baba...tum sarko uleolo....ami tumchea pasot....amchea bhurgeam pasot fokot poixe zoddunk lagleat....amchea avoi-bapai lagim poixe chodd naslele punn tannim bore molache sonskar amkam dile....Tech molache sonskar tumkam diunche bodlek ami apsvarthi axeche gulam zale....bogos amkam baba

PRIEST: Lord, I ask your pardon. I have a vocation to make you and your life, real and tangible, to my flock. How easily have I slipped into a bubble of convenience, wickedness & deception! How cleverly have I used, abused, and misused those who trust in me! So many of them have gone astray because I no longer inspire them! I have lost those you had entrusted unto me, O Father! Destroy this hard shell of disguise that I choose to live in! Make me live and lead others to follow a path of truth and goodness.

ARCHITECT: Jezuchea khursa mullint ami portum-ia...Umkolltelea Soddvonarachim utram amkam nirop ditelim...Jezuche avoiche bhaxen....Ankvar Marieche bhaxen ami guptim tachim utram amchea kallzamnim ballgum-ia...tednam ami-i Marieche bhaxen kalljidar Devachea Kaklutiche missionar zatelim. Mother Mary inspires us to inspire one another.

[Mother Mary emerges from the other end of the cross and moves slowly and solemnly towards the cross] [All characters are awestruck]

[SONG 25: Jesus rose on the cross]

MOTHER MARY:

The sword pierced my Heart
When I saw my son on that cross
But I chose to remain
Your handmaid O my God

On that shameful wooden cross
They crucified my boy
But my Jesus forgave them
And rose as Christ our Lord

[All characters rally around Mother Mary...and the choir sings] A movie clip shows abstract effects of light emerging from darkness... resurrection emerging from death

MINISTER: Ulo amchea soddvonnaracho.... kanar gheum-ia...Dubhav apsvartponn soddun, Jezuche niz xis khoxe...Mogan jieum-ia. Yes.....neither will I go back to my rotten ways....nor will I give up on life? I will get back to Christ....Yes, I want to be there for the Lord in the world today. I pray that You be there too!

[SONG 26: RISE AND CELEBRATE]

MEN:

Every temptation to sin
Every trial we will be in
Is an opportunity
To rise above sin and pain
Conquer death and declare victory

CHOIR:

Every temptation to sin
Every trial we will be in
Is an opportunity
To rise above sin and pain
Conquer death and declare victory

WOMEN:

Don't let sin hunt you down (2)
(cf Numbers 32/23)
By the death of the lamb
We have heaven already won

CHOIR:

ALLELUIA…ALLELUIA…ALLELUIA.

PLAY FOUR

RISE AND WALK

.... towards Peace

A reflection on human pursuit of Peace

LENTEN MUSICAL

शुभ संदेश
SHANTINAGAR - BHOPAL
PRESENTS
उठो और चलो.....
......शांति की ओर
RISE AND WALK.... towards PEACE
A reflection on human pursuit of Peace
A LENTEN MUSICAL THRILLER!
02 APRIL 2023
06:30 PM
VENUE: PRAKASH VIDYALAYA GROUNDS, SHANTINAGAR - BHOPAL
येसु क्रूस पर भी अपनी शांति को कैसे नहीं खोए ?
आइये हम येसु के साथ उठें और चले और अपनी आंतरिक शांति का पता लगाएं
A Journey into one's soul
to rekindle the gift of Peace within
and live in peace as one Cosmic Family
A GOSPEL ECHO......
HOSTS: Shantinagar Parish, BHOPAL

The characters

The Hindi version of this play was staged at Prakash Vidyalaya grounds, Shantinagar - Bhopal on Sunday, 2 April, 2023, and at St Joseph Co-Ed school grounds, Arera Colony on Sunday, 16 April, 2023 with the following Cast:

NARRATOR 1	Kashmir
NARRATOR 2	Karnita
MOTHER 1	Anand Prabha Xalxo
MOTHER 2	Callista
MOTHER 3	Philomena
FATHER 1	Ajit Xalxo
FATHER 2, CRIMINAL (left)	Rohit
FATHER 3 (POLICEMAN)	Anand Xalxo
CHILD 1	Geniys Lakra, Shreya
CHILD 2	Srinivas Behra
CHILD 3	Paul Ekka
CHILD 4	Abraham Sadom
CHILD 5	Anshika Xalxo
CHILD 6	Mary Kalpana Xalxo
TEACHER 1	Ayushi Ekka/Roshni
TEACHER 2	Prachi kujur
TEACHER 3	Laxmi Dhurve, Rozy Daniel
TEACHER 4	Abhineeth Kujur
PRINCIPAL	Olima Dungdung
MANAGER	Abhay
BUSINESS MAN	Aseem Xalxo
ENGINEER, SOLDIER 2	Anuragh Lakra
DOCTOR 1	Deepika, Anusha
DOCTOR 2, CRIMINAL (Right)	Roshan
DOCTOR 3	Archana Paraste
DOCTOR 4, SIMON OF CYRENE	Ankit Toppo
NURSE	Jennifer Kujur

POLITICIAN, SOLDIER 1	Priyanshu Ekka
LAWYER 1, CHIEF PRIEST 2	Ashish
LAWYER 2	Ankit Kerketta
CLERK (JAIN)	Ramsila xalxo
JESUS 1, 2	Anuragh Kujur, Aryan Lakra,
SATAN	Deepika Xalxo
MOTHER MARY	Amita Xalxo
MARY MAGDALENE	Ankita Xalxo (Jr), Preethi
MARY (mother of James/Joseph)	Vinita Kujur
SALOME	Reshma Minj
JOHN	Prince Kujur
JUDAS ISCARIOT	Fr. Praful
PETER	Prashant Lakra
VERONICA	Pratigya, Rozy
CENTURION	Abhineeth
CHIEF PRIEST 1	Vineeth
CROWD – path to Calvary	
CHOIR	

SONGS (VOICE-OVER) – choral group

SONG NO	**CHARACTER**	**VOICE**	**ACTOR**
1	SOLO 1	Megha	Roshni
	SOLO 2	Sugandi	Rosy
	SOLO 3	Sewan	Rohit
2	POLITICIAN	Rio	Priyanshu
	LAWYER	Prabhat	Ashish
	DOCTOR 4	Valerian	Ankit Toppo
	ENGINEER	Habil	Anuragh Lakra
4	DOCTOR 1	Sugandi	Deepika Topno
	CHRISTIAN	Sewan	Ajit
5	JESUS	Valerian	Anuragh, Aryan, Sourabh
6	VERONICA	Sudipa	Pratigya Toppo
7	JUDAS	Rio	Preetam Toppo sfx
8	PETER	Prabhat	Prashant Lakra

9	MAGDALENE	Megha	Ankita Xalxo (Jr), Preeti
10	SATAN	Allan	Deepika Xalxo
11	JESUS	Valerian	Saurabh, Aryan

Concept, Script, Music, and Direction **ALLAN TAVARES** SFX

Music Arrangement by **RIO FERNANDES**

Hostel Choir direction by **Lucy Tonglim, Roshni Sadom**

Translation into Hindi by **Students of ICJ, Bhopal; Deepika Xalxo, Roshni Sadom; Abhishek Xalxo, Ameeta Xalxo**

Costume & Makeup Management by **Sr. Sudipa, Sr. Sayuja, Sr. Jeevan Lata, Raymond Fernandes sfx, Roshni Sadom**

Sets Management & Stage marshalling by **Praful Indwar sfx, Pratik John Gangle, Abhay, Abhishek**

Light Effects Management by **Madhan, Aseem, and Dharmesh Singh**

Sound Management by **Allan Tavares sfx**

Produced by **SHUBHSANDESH SHANTINAGAR, BHOPAL**

The Troupe of 'Rise and Walk'

Hostel children singing in the choir for 'Rise and Walk.'

The playback singers for 'Rise and Walk.'

Most Rev. Duvairaj svd, Archbishop of Bhopal, graced the occasion

Prelude

KARNITA (NARRATOR 1): (*enters from the center.... spot on him*) Our world stands tormented by conflict and wars!

KASMIR (NARRATOR 2): (*enters from the right.... spot on him*) How do we rekindle the gifts of God within each one's soul? The gifts of Love, Joy, Faith, Hope, and Communion as one cosmic family!

KARNITA (NARRATOR 1): Could we pause for a moment from our mad rush and return to the 'inner room' of our hearts and listen to the deepest yearnings of our hearts!

KASMIR (NARRATOR 2): Yes! Could we listen to our heart yearning for Peace!

[SONG 01: LET MY HEART REST IN PEACE]

CHOIR: We are yearning
We are seeking
We are searching…. for Peace (2)
MEGA: My heart is made for you, O God
SEVAN: My heart is a womb of Love
SUGANDI: My heart is a Temple of your Spirit
CHORAL: My heart is made for you my God (2)
CHOIR: We are yearning
We are seeking
We are searching…. for Peace (2)
MEGA: Then, why O God, do you set me free
To choose against your will

Why do you allow me, O God
To ruin my heart with sin?
SEVAN (SOLO 2): My thoughts are too small
To comprehend you, O God

My feelings are too raw
I need to mature

SUGANDI (SOLO 3): Why can't I, out of freedom
Just do good to everyone?
Why can't I, out of freedom
Give up what is wrong

CHORAL: And when I am right away doing good, then there is Peace in my World (2)

CHOIR: We are yearning
We are seeking
We are searching.... for Peace (2)

Scene one: A marketplace.

Music of Tempest

A group of parents, children, teachers, managers, businessmen, builders, architects/engineers, doctors & nurses, sitting adjacent to each other, busy in themselves. A group of religious leaders was seated a little away in the convention.

ANAND PRABHA (MOTHER 1): (serving tea) They say that a family is a cradle of civilization.

CALLISTA (MOTHER 2): Yes, all that is good in the world happens when a family is good and strong.

PHILOMENA (MOTHER 3): My parents did not go to school, but they inspired me to be good and to do good in every situation.

AJIT (FATHER 1): So, what then is going wrong now? I am educated, my wife is educated, and we just don't understand how to raise our children.

ANAND PRABHA (MOTHER 1): I agree with you. It is so difficult to understand our growing children. They seem to be hiding things from us. Why don't they trust us?

GENI (CHILD 1): Mom, we do trust you. We do want to tell you everything. But, do you have the time?

PRINCE (CHILD 4): Dad, I think you and Mom never got educated to be parents. Yes, you are literate, highly literate, but you know very little about me as your child.

JYOTI (CHILD 5): I am born to be different, different from every other child and even different from you.

SRINIVAS (CHILD 2): I sometimes wonder why my parents force me to go for tuitions, when I could have managed alone with guidance from my teachers. Don't you, our parents, believe in us, your children?

PAUL (CHILD 3): We no longer eat our meals together, as a family, talking to each other.

CHRISTOPHER (FATHER 2): Is it the mobile phone that is keeping us away from each other, as a family?

PRABHAT (FATHER 3): Maybe yes. Maybe no. But we certainly need to restore 'Peace and Love' in our families!

[SONG 02: LET MY FAMILY REST IN PEACE]

CHOIR: We are yearning
We are seeking
We are searching…. for Peace (2)
MEGA: My heart is made for you, O God
SEVAN: My heart is a womb of Love
SUGANDI): My heart is a Temple of your Spirit
CHORAL: My heart is made for you, my God (2)
CHOIR: We are yearning
We are seeking
We are searching…. for Peace (2)
SUDIPA (MOTHER 1): Help me raise my children
Whom I bore in my womb
Help me see in every child
Your very image, O God (2)
PRABHAT (FATHER 3): Help me make them walk
On the right path, O God
May I inspire them
Make my 'love' go strong (2)
JYOTI (CHILD 5): OH, my parents, I love you
I do want to trust you.
Guide me to choose what is right
And do what is good
CHORAL: And when we right away do good, there'll be Peace in our World (2)
CHOIR: We are yearning

We are seeking
We are searching.... for Peace (2)

AMEETA (TEACHER 1): A school is a second home for a child

DEEPIKA (TEACHER 2): Parents trust teachers to let their children grow with the right knowledge, right skills, and right attitude.

JEEVAN LATA - TEACHER 3: It is a joy for a teacher to discover something very precious and different in every child.

ABHINEETH- TEACHER 4: It is a challenge for a teacher to look and believe in the strengths of every child, even if they are not clearly seen, rather than see and be discouraged by the visible weakness of every child.

DIVYA- CHILD 6: That's the reason why we love our teachers. Not everyone is called to be a teacher.

SRINIVAS - CHILD 2: That's why teaching is more of a vocation than a profession.

AMEETA - TEACHER 1: However, today, a teacher is under stress. The government pays teachers fat salaries and expects us to cover a heavy syllabus.

DEEPIKA - TEACHER 2: Yes, because there is a lot of money in teaching for a half-day job, we love being teachers.

JEEVAN LATA - TEACHER 3: And we try to somehow cover the syllabus.

ABHINEETH- - TEACHER 4: Our attention today is shifting from the children whom we are supposed to love and transform, to money and syllabus.

ANIL - MANAGER: When our attention is only on making more money out of our schools, then we are never at peace. We lose the opportunity to transform the present generation of students into a promising civilization of citizens. Instead, we end up running a business in the name of education.

***CELINE* - PRINCIPAL**: How do we restore Peace & Love & Hope into our educational institutions?

[SONG 03: O CHILD OF MINE]

CHOIR: We are yearning
We are seeking
We are searching…. for Peace (2)
MEGA: My heart is made for you, O God
SEVAN (SOLO 2): My heart is a womb of Love
SUGANDI: My heart is a Temple of your Spirit
CHORAL: My heart is made for you, my God (2)
CHOIR: We are yearning
We are seeking
We are searching…. for Peace (2)
JEEVAN LATA - TEACHER 3:
O child of mine (2)
Let me find in you
Splendour Divine (2)
VALERIAN: Let me rejoice and run my school
Let me rejoice in this Gift of God
May my school train every student
To be leading citizens of the world
DIVYA - CHILD 6: OH, my dear teachers
O my dear teachers
Inspire me with values
Help me pursue Excellence!
CHORAL: And when we pursue what is good,
There'll be Peace in our World (2)
CHOIR: We are yearning
We are seeking

We are searching.... for Peace (2)

***RIO* - BUSINESSMAN**: Well, if you think that 'Teaching' has become a 'business', then I, the businessman, am to be blamed. I have made 'business' the most desirable pursuit for every man & woman in the world. Everyone wants to run a business today!

JOSEPH - BUILDER 1: Earlier, we used to think that business is run only in marketplaces, but today, even we builders are running the biggest business!

RACHANA - ARCHITECT 1: As an architect, today I am tempted to design as many buildings, since the more buildings that I design, the more money!

SUGANDI - DOCTOR 1: Isn't it sad that we, doctors, too, have fallen into the business trap? We, who were respected as Gods for saving lives, today would also like to treat as many patients, not for the love of the patients but to make more money.

ROSHAN- DOCTOR 2: Or work in as many hospitals to make more money.

ARCHANA - DOCTOR 3: How else do we make up for the lakhs of rupees we have spent to study medicine?

VALERIAN - DOCTOR 4: So, it's a vicious cycle. The medical colleges run a business & therefore we pay more to be doctors & so we run clinics & hospitals to make money too!

JENNIFER - NURSE 1: Are our hospitals lifesaving or business houses?

ANURAG - ENGINEER: As an engineer, I am tempted to ask: Are the buildings I design safe to live in? Or if they are safe, are they affordable for the poor?

KASMIR - NARRATOR 1: ......and it is not just about engineers, architects, builders, doctors, nurses, businessmen, teachers. Everyone is allured today to measure their success in life by the money they make! Every profession is becoming a business!

KARNITA - NARRATOR 2: We are in a serious pursuit of 'money' and 'pleasures of the world'.

KASMIR - NARRATOR 1: We are all seeking either 'money' or 'honey'.

KARNITA - NARRATOR 2: But will these very attractive and desirable yearnings truly give me peace?

[SONG 04: NEITHER 'MONEY' NOR 'HONEY']

CHOIR: We are all after 'money–money–money.'
We are all after 'honey–honey–honey.'
But neither money nor honey gives us peace – (2)

RIO - BUSINESS MAN: What then brings me peace
If not, the honey that's so tasty
What then makes my soul content
If not, the money in my bank

ALEX - BUILDER 2:
What then will make me work like crazy
If not, my future security

CHORAL: What then will bring me Peace?

CHOIR: We are all after 'money–money–money.'
We are all after 'honey–honey–honey.'
But neither money nor honey gives us peace – (2)

VALERIAN - DOCTOR 4:
Desiring a partner of my dreams
Will it make my world truly happy?
Helping the less fortunate
Is it part of my business dream

RACHANA/CELINE – ARCHITECT 1/2:

The great things I want to make
Will it make my world a safer place?

CHORAL: What then will bring me Peace?

CHOIR: We are all after 'money–money–money.'
We are all after 'honey–honey–honey.'
But neither money nor honey gives us peace – (2)

CHORAL: Only when we pursue what is good, there'll be
Peace in our World (2)

CHOIR: We are yearning
We are seeking
We are searching.... for Peace (2)

KASMIR - NARRATOR 1: Somewhere, somehow, we are chasing wrong things! I think it will be good for all of us to meet the 'gurus' of our religions. Maybe they will have answers to our questions.

KARNITA - NARRATOR 2: Infact, the gurus themselves have gathered for a convention, trying to understand how to set right what seems to be going wrong. Let us meet them!

[SONG 05: O GURUJIS]

CHOIR: Help us, O Gurujis
Guide us to inner peace

SEVAN - GURUJI 1:

We are tempted to ask you
How much are you ready <u>to pay us?</u> (3)

PRABHAT - GURUJI 2:

Don't be surprised

Because we have made religion too
- a business (3)

VALERIAN – GURUJI 3:

The more you pay us, the better our service will be (3)

CHORAL: So, it is time that we sing a common song
Even we, in the name of religion,
have gone wrong (2)

CHOIR: It's time to change
It's time to change our hearts and minds
Let us join our hearts and hands
Let us make our world – a home for Peace!

KASMIR - NARRATOR 1: O Gurujis, you are guardians of our religion. You certainly cannot be businessmen or businesswomen!

KARNITA - NARRATOR 2: And you cannot blame it on being human.

KASMIR - NARRATOR 1: It's great to see you come to a humble understanding that we all need to change.

KARNITA - NARRATOR 2: Tell us how each religion inspires inner peace.

KASMIR - NARRATOR 1: Please rekindle in us, once again, the flame of 'Peace.'

SANJEET - BUDDHIST MONK: Buddha says, 'Meditate and attain inner peace and express it as 'maitri' (loving kindness), 'karuna' (compassion), 'mudita' (sympathetic joy), and 'upeksa' (equanimity).

PRIYANSHU - MULLAH: In Islam, peace is denoted by four Quranic terms: 'Amn' implies that to be at peace is to be without fear, 'silm' implies that peace comes through surrender to the will of Allah, 'salam' implies that the source of peace is Allah, 'sulk' implies that peace means the end of all war. We are not to take Allah's name as an excuse against peace.

ANUMOL - HINDU SWAMI: Bhagwad Gita gives us a peace formula: one attains peace by knowing God as (Lord, Provider, Friend, Benefactor) existing in one's heart through whom we perceive everything. The Bhagwat Gita is a doctrine on Peace and should not be misinterpreted as a doctrine of war because it was dictated on a battlefield!

ISHA - BAHAI: As a Bahai, I believe that wars will end when women who are mothers enter politics and world affairs.... for which mother would want her sons and daughters to be sent to the battlefield?

PRASHANTH - SIKH GRANTHI: As a Sikh, I believe that 'Dharam' requires me to rise above greed, lust, violence & lack of compassion so as to end pain & suffering in society, then only will there be peace.

SANDEEP -JAIN MONK: Yes, that's true! Peace comes through self-conquest. Therefore, as a 'Jain' I am 'Jina' – a conqueror! Then only can I practice 'Ahimsa', overcoming aversion, practice 'Apanigraha', overcoming attachments, to come to a state of 'Anekantvada' (peaceful equanimity).

ANKIT - CHRISTIAN: For Jesus, peace was the sweet fragrance of 'sacrifice' that one willingly makes of oneself so that the Holy name of God – as a loving Father – be glorified through humble & joyful service of the needy and the poor.

KASMIR - NARRATOR 1: Holy lives of a few men & women gave birth to religions! How beautifully each one of you brought to our attention that every religion is a path of peace! And yet, how many wars and how much violence we get to see in our world in the name of religion!

KARNITA - NARRATOR 2: Could we make the lives of the holy men & women...who inspired religions to be born....

yes, could their lives be made livable again!

KASMIR - NARRATOR 1: We will need to have a closer peep into each of their lives!

KARNITA - NARRATOR 2: We could begin with Jesus of Nazareth, as this time of the year is the Lenten season during which Christians meditate on the sufferings and death of Jesus.

SANJEET - BUDDHIST MONK: Yes, I would like to have a closer look at Jesus. I am always fascinated by how Jesus managed to 'rise' and 'walk' out of the worldly temptations which Satan threw at him.

PRASHANT - SIKH GRANTHI: Jesus' life was a perfect example of real 'Dharam'. His 'life of compassion' just inspires me.

RAMSILA - JAIN MONK: Jesus' life was a life of self-conquest. He practiced 'Ahimsa', 'Apanigraha', and therefore was 'peaceful even when taken to die on a cross'. I would certainly join in meditating on his life.

PRIYANSHU - MULLAH: What is it that made Jesus be at peace, even in the worst of trials? Could Jesus inspire you and me to 'Rise & Walk' every time I am knocked down?

ABHAY - HINDU SWAMI: Yes... How could Jesus of Nazareth not lose his inner peace on his way to Calvary? What is it that made Jesus so peacefully 'rise' and 'walk' to Calvary?

KASMIR - NARRATOR 1: Let us 'RISE' & 'WALK' with Jesus ....and perhaps we may find our own inner Peace!

[SONG 06: Let us learn from Jesus]

CHOIR: Let's learn from Jesus (3)
Jesus of Nazareth, Our Lord Jesus Christ

SUGANDI -DOCTOR 1:
He started His mission saying, 'Repent.'
He said 'Repent, for the Kingdom of God is at hand
He called a few to be His apostles
And a few more to be His disciples
He sent them two-by-two
to proclaim the good news

CHOIR: Let's learn from Jesus (3)
Jesus of Nazareth, Our Lord Jesus Christ

SEVAN - CHRISTIAN:
Jesus preached through mighty wonders
He made the deaf hear & He made the dumb to speak
He made the lame to 'Rise & Walk'.
He cleansed the lepers…He drove out the evil spirits
He raised the sinners out of sin and shame
He made the dead to 'Rise & Walk'.

CHOIR: Let's learn from Jesus (3)
Jesus of Nazareth
Who breathed unto His apostles
His Own Peace.

A scene from 'Rise and Walk':
Jesus falling while carrying the cross

Scene Two: Wilderness.

Music of the Tempest
Jesus in the wilderness, leaning on a rock, praying to God His Father. Satan mocks Jesus and devises strategies to tempt Jesus.

[SONG 07: Abba Father]

CHOIR: Abba Father, who art in Heaven
Thy Kingdom come.
Thy will be done
VALERIAN - JESUS:
Abba…My Father
Holy…be your name.
Give me today…my daily bread (2)
Abba…My Father
Holy…be your name.
Forgive me my sins…as I forgive..
Forgive those who sinned against me
Abba…My Father
Holy…be your name.
Do not bring me…to the test
Deliver me…from all evil
Abba…My Father
Holy…be your name.
CHOIR: Abba Father, who art in Heaven
Thy Kingdom come.
Thy will be done

SATAN: (*laughing mockingly and loudly*) O man Jesus…hungry for forty days…and still talking about the daily bread. Did your Father in heaven give you your daily bread? If you are so beloved to your God, then He should not keep you hungry for forty long days…. I'll tell you what! Enough is enough! Use your own power! Your words have power. Say to these stones, 'Be bread, and these stones will become bread indeed! (*Satan is continuing to draw Jesus' attention in mute, while narrators' comment*)

KASMIR - NARRATOR 1: Hey! Satan is tempting a very hungry Jesus!

KARNITA - NARRATOR 2: I am reminded of the number of times when I think that I am denied what I deserve from my very own…and I am tempted to prove a point by using my education, talents, influence, and all other strengths to grab power. I am tempted to order stones to become bread and satiate my hunger. (*Focus back on Satan*)

SATAN: It makes no sense to remain hungry for so many days. Just order these stones to become bread!

VALERIAN - JESUS: I know what I am doing. I don't need to order stones to be bread. 'Man does not live on bread alone but on every word that comes from God.

SATAN: Don't take me wrong, Jesus. I was only concerned about you. Well…inspite of your hunger, if you can still 'rise and walk', I would like to show you something interesting!

VALERIAN - JESUS: Yes, I can walk. Show me what you want me to see.

SATAN: O man, you walk so strong…inspite of being terribly hungry. Your gait, your strides, your looks…You make one complete package of a handsome, young, eligible bachelor boy! (*laughs*) I am sure women will fall for you……and you should just take a plunge…. nothing will go wrong for you…. well, here we are at the edge of the cliff…..Just jump down and feel the pleasure of your heavenly angels sent by your Father in heaven, who will catch you mid-air. Nothing will happen to you.

VALERIAN -JESUS: I don't need to test my God who loves me as a beloved and whom I love so dearly. I don't need to do something stupid like jumping off the cliff. I am happy doing simple things each day with utmost love!

SATAN: Oh yes…You are so right….one should never test God! I admire your allegiance to God. I am sure your God is indeed pleased with you. What a *Devbhakt*? And yet I advise you to be practical. You are going to start your own venture now, with chosen men and women. You need money for such a venture! And I would be more than willing to help you out. Do you see that beautiful city there? It belongs to me. Just for once, bow before me….and I'll give all of it to you. (*Satan is continuing to draw Jesus' attention in mute, while the narrator comments*)

KASMIR - NARRATOR 1: What deceiving temptations. I am reminded of how difficult it is for me to choose between 'material comforts' and 'total allegiance to God'.

SATAN: Hey, man! I am very honest. I don't like cheating! It's a pure bargain. Just bow once before me, and that city is yours.

VALERIAN - JESUS: Enough is enough, Satan. Begone! I choose to worship my God and serve Him alone.

KARNITA - NARRATOR 2: I think…that's the difference between Jesus and me, between Jesus and us.

***KASMIR - NARRATOR 1*:** What do you think of the final temptation of Jesus, when he walked to Calvary? Do you think Satan would just let him be?

KARNITA - NARRATOR 2: Yes, it would be inspiring to walk along with Jesus to Calvary

Scene Three: Way to Calvary

Music of tempest…combined with Motet.
Jesus fallen on the ground, under the weight of the wood that he is made to carry. John is attending to Jesus. Mary, Mother of Jesus, is watching along with Mary Magdalene and his mother's sister, Mary, the wife of Clopas. Soldiers are searching for someone to carry the cross. They find Simon of Cyrene. High Priests are staring at Jesus. Satan is plotting!

MANISH - JOHN: *(trying to lift the cross of wood from Jesus' body)* O Master! This piece of wood is so heavy. Must you carry it? You don't deserve this punishment, which is meant for criminals. You are innocent. You only went about doing good…. some of them are here *(pointing to some familiar faces of people whom Jesus had healed)* …and they are just watching you go through this undeserving ordeal! We have all become helpless at a time when you need us! We are not able to help you. *(trying to lift the cross)* I can't even lift this from you.

SATAN: *(mockingly)* Oh, yes, Jesus! All whom you had done good to, have chosen to be bad to you! Ha! Ha! Ha!...... Well, John, I don't think you can be of big help to your Master…

(Mother Mary goes to her son and helps him…Jesus rises to walk…soldiers bring Simon of Cyrene to help carry the cross…. Satan reacts…. he does not want anyone to help Jesus)

Hey! Hey! Why are you trying to help him…. let him try walking it alone!

***KASMIR - NARRATOR 1*:** Look at this mother. Mother of Jesus. She speaks no words to her son that we can hear, and he makes no complaint to his mother, and yet she speaks to his heart. She says everything needed to make her son, Jesus, 'Rise and Walk' again.

(Veronica comes running to wipe the face of Jesus)

[SONG 08: O people, how could you be cruel]

SUDIPA - VERONICA: *(to Jesus)*

Oh Master, see what they've done to you.
You've left on this towel
A picture of Love – so true!
O people, how could you be so cruel
To this man of God, who helped you
- who blessed you - who loved you!

CHOIR: O people, how could you be so cruel
To this man of God, who helped you - who blessed you - who loved you!

SUDIPA - VERONICA: *(to Mother Mary)*

Oh Mother, I just can't bear to see your pain.
You walk with your son with such courage
O people, how could you be so cruel
To this man of God, who helped you –
who blessed you - who loved you!

CHOIR: O people, how could you be so cruel
To this man of God, who helped you - who blessed you - who loved you!

SUDIPA - VERONICA: *(to John & other women)*

Oh, brother John, O dear sisters
Where are the others gone?
Where are all those whom he called his own?
OH, people, how could you be so cruel
To this man of God, who helped you - who blessed you - who loved you!

CHOIR: O people, how could you be so cruel
To this man of God, who helped you - who blessed you - who loved you!

SUDIPA - VERONICA: *(to Jesus and Mother of Jesus)*
Oh, dear Jesus, O dear Mother, I adore you
CHOIR: Oh, dear Jesus, O dear Mother, I adore you

KARNITA - NARRATOR 2: That was indeed brave of that woman – Veronica!

KASMIR - NARRATOR 1: And she asked a very relevant question: Where is Peter and the rest of the Apostles? *(The narrator's attention is diverted to a man who is pacing towards them)* I can see someone running in here!

KARNITA - NARRATOR 2: That is Judas Iscariot, who sold Jesus to these High Priests, for a mere thirty pieces of Silver. What more has this betrayer come here for?

[SONG 09: I have betrayed my Master]

RIO - JUDAS ISCARIOT:
What have I done? I am in real confusion!
What have I done? I think I betrayed Him.
I had thought I would make some money
Out of what these priests offered me.
Because I knew He was a son of God
Therefore, I thought, He would somehow set himself free!
But nothing (3) as such is happening.
He is just walking, struggling, rising, and walking
I don't want him to die on Calvary
Can somebody help him (3)
I have betrayed my Master for the sake of money!

(JESUS FALLS THE SECOND TIME, Judas Iscariot runs towards Jesus to help. Soldiers don't allow him to come to Jesus. Mother Mary goes to her son and helps him…Jesus rises to walk…The soldiers make

Simon of Cyrene help carry the cross.... Satan reacts.... he does not want anyone to help Jesus)

CHOIR: What have you done? (2)
Judas Iscariot! You betrayed your Master
Repent, O dear brother!

SATAN: *(mockingly)* Ha! Ha! Ha! Did you listen to that, Jesus.... One of your very own has betrayed you. Ha! Ha! Ha! I thought you were a wise man. You should be making better choices. Judas is frantically asking for help....and for you. Who do you think can help you?
Even your God – your Father, whom you loved so much - will not help you now!

(JESUS FALLS THE THIRD TIME, Mother Mary goes to her son and helps him...Jesus rises to walk.... Satan reacts.... he does not want anyone to help Jesus...and yet he wants him to rise and walk)

SATAN: *(to Jesus)* Hey, Jesus! Don't just keep falling. I want you to 'rise and walk' to Calvary. When they hang you on that cross, I want you to curse your God and die like a criminal .... So what... if you were innocent? I am waiting to see the miserable death of a holy man of God!

KASMIR - NARRATOR 1: That's terrible! Satan wants Jesus to 'rise and walk' and die a miserable death! WILL JESUS LOSE HIS PEACE ON THE CROSS?

KARNITA - NARRATOR 2: Hey! See! It's Peter there! watching Jesus from a distance? Why is he not coming to help his Master? He seems to be saying something to Jesus. Let's listen to him

[SONG 10: Rise and Walk O Master]

PRABHAT - PETER:

O Master, you were right!
I have denied you without a fight! (2)
When I raised the sword, you made me withdraw
When I needed to be there by your side
I am on a run, out of fright!
All the promises I made have just evaporated
You called me Caiaphas – the solid rock
But here I am - a coward!

PRABHAT - PETER:

O Master, you were right!
I have denied you without a fight! (2)
Yes, I don't have the guts, O Master
And I don't want to give up
Every drop of your blood, O Master
I want to make it count
I will gather our brothers back
And wait for your return
<u>Rise and Walk O Master,</u>
<u>May the Will of God be done!</u> (2)

KASMIR - NARRATOR 1: Peter reminds me of myself. I honestly want to do some real big things for God, but somehow, I fall short….and I fall! and the challenge is to 'Rise and Walk, every time I fail and fall! Peter exhorts his Master to 'Rise and Walk' and do the Will of God

(Jesus reaches the top of Calvary, soldiers strip him and prepare to nail him to the cross…. Mary Magdalene cannot bear to see this…. she wants to cover Jesus' body and pleads to the soldiers not to hurt her Master)

MEGHA - MARY MAGDALENE: Don't do this to Him! Please leave Him alone! Don't hurt Him! I need Him! You need Him! We all need Him!

(Soldiers push her aside. Mary, the mother of James, goes and picks Mary Magdalene)

[SONG 11: My Saviour, My Jesus]

MEGHA -MARY MAGDALENE:

Here is the man who loved me!
Here is the man who healed me!
Here is the man who freed me!
My Saviour, Jesus my Lord

CHOIR: Here is the man who loved us!
Here is the man who healed us!
Here is the man who freed us!
Our Saviour, Jesus our Lord

MEGHA - MARY MAGDALENE:

Thank you, O lord for healing me
Thank you for saving me from sin
Thank you, Lord, for loving me
Thank you, O Lord, for your Love.

MEGHA - MARY MAGDALENE:

Here is the man who loved me!
Here is the man who healed me!
Here is the man who freed me!
My Saviour, Jesus my Lord

CHOIR: Here is the man who loved us!
Here is the man who healed us!

Here is the man who freed us!
Our Saviour, Jesus our Lord

MEGHA - MARY MAGDALENE:
O Father, give your son, your strength
To bear this unbearable pain
O Father, thank you for giving us your son
Hold him close to your heart

MEGHA - MARY MAGDALENE:
Here is the man who loved me!
Here is the man who healed me!
Here is the man who freed me!
My Saviour, Jesus my Lord

CHOIR: Here is the man who loved us!
Here is the man who healed us!
Here is the man who freed us!
Our Saviour, Jesus our Lord

(Music continues)

SATAN: Yes, the death of Jesus will break the hearts of many! I wonder why Peter wanted Jesus to 'Rise and Walk'? Does he want his master to die? I would certainly want Jesus to die...and see him lose his peace.... And curse his God before he dies!

KASMIR - NARRATOR 1: That's terrible! Satan does not have any decency, even in the face of this horrible torture that this innocent Jesus is going through!

KARNITA - NARRATOR 2: And Mary, the mother of Jesus is so silent...she chooses to be silent. She again ponders it all, in the cave of her heart.

KASMIR - NARRATOR 1: And that is such a profound

influence on Jesus. He too chooses to walk in total contemplation, silent and resilient as he transforms the dreadful path to Calvary into a path of inner peace and purpose

(Curtain opens and Jesus is seen hanging on the cross with two criminals on either side. Soldiers mock at him, Mary – mother of Jesus along with John, Mary Magdalene and his mother's sister, Mary the wife of Clopas are at the foot of the cross)

SATAN: Alright! It's show time now. I want to make it real difficult for this man, Jesus....... Hey Jesus, you saved others, who will save you now?

HABIL - SOLDIER 1: If you are the son of God, then come down now. Ha! Ha! Ha!

PRAFUL - CRIMINAL (LEFT): Save yourself and save me too! Prove that you are the son of God.

JESUS: I THIRST

ALEX - SOLDIER 2: Hey! He says he thirsts. Give him some dirty gall mixed in vinegar. Perhaps that will make him jump down from the cross.

(Soldier serves gall to Jesus, which Jesus refuses to drink)

SATAN: How does it feel dear Jesus.... thirsty...ridiculed? Call it 'the end'. You certainly have a reason to be angry with your God. He is so unjust towards you! Show it aloud......curse him loudly!

JESUS: FATHER FORGIVE THEM FOR THEY KNOW NOT WHAT THEY DO!

SATAN: Come on man! There is no space for holiness now! It's time up! Its time to just curse your God and die!

SUNIT - CRIMINAL (RIGHT): Jesus, I know you are a good man. You don't deserve this death. However, you've willingly accepted it to save wretched souls like me. Please remember me in your kingdom.

JESUS: YOU SHALL BE WITH ME TODAY, IN PARADISE.

SATAN: What is happening here? You are not supposed to be goodie…goodie anymore….

JESUS: JOHN, YOUR MOTHER! MOTHER, YOUR SON!

SATAN: Oh no! This man Jesus is a hard nut to crack!

JESUS: O FATHER, IT IS ALL ACCOMPLISHED. MAY YOUR WILL BE DONE!

(Satan is desperate because Jesus is so calmly blessing people from the cross)

[SONG 12:] [AT PEACE, HANGING ON A CROSS?]

SATAN: No! (14)
Something is going wrong! (2)
You should be cursing God
When you are hanging on that cross
You should be losing your peace, man
Instead of whispering blessings!
How can you hang on a cross
and still be at peace?
No! (14)
Something is going wrong! (2)

[SONG 13:] [I SURRENDER MY SPIRIT]

VALERIAN - JESUS:
I SURRENDER MY SPIRIT
UNTO YOUR HANDS O MY GOD! (2)
I seek your blessings on one and all
Who followed me for your kingdom

Bless O Father, those who crucify me
For they know not what they are doing.
Thank you for helping me 'Rise and Walk'
Out of every temptation.
I 'Rise and Walk' now across death
Into your eternal kingdom
I SURRENDER MY SPIRIT
UNTO YOUR HANDS O MY GOD! (2)

(Jesus dies.... sound of earthquake, strong wind)
(Soldier pierces the side of Jesus, and water and blood flow)

***SEVAN* - *CENTURION*:** This man truly was the Son of God!
(Soldier serves gall to Jesus, which Jesus refuses to drink)

***SATAN*:** Yes, I admit! He has proved by his life as well as by his death that he is indeed the Son of God! His example of pure holiness in the worst of what I could throw at him can now be such an inspiration for all human beings to overcome my temptations and live beyond sin and death! Oh no! I cannot let this happen! *(Satan runs out, ranting in utter frustration)*

***KARNITA* - *NARRATOR 2*:** *(enters from the center.... spot on him)* I remember how Jesus, even as a child, chose to 'rise' above the mundane and 'walk' the distant mile, to understand His Father's Business. In his ministry, Jesus made the sick and even the dead, to 'rise' and 'walk'......and now Jesus so peacefully chooses to 'rise' above sin to 'walk' across death into eternity as 'The Risen Lord'.

[SONG 14] [RISE & WALK WITH JESUS]

MEGA/CELINE - SOLO 1:

He is Humble, He is meek

VALERIAN/SEVAN - SOLO 2:

He is loving, He is forgiving

CHORAL: He heals and blesses those who seek him (2)

SUDIPA/JEEVAN - SOLO 3:

He didn't stop loving, even when it hurt Him

RIO/PRABHAT - SOLO 4:

He didn't stop blessing. He was at Peace

CHORAL: Rise and Walk with Jesus and find Peace (2)
CHOIR: Rise and Walk with Jesus and find Peace (2)

MEGA/CELINE - SOLO 1:

Let us be humble, let us be meek

VALERIAN/SEVAN - SOLO 2:

Let us be loving, let us forgive

CHORAL: Let us heal and bless our fellow beings (2)

SUDIPA/JEEVAN - SOLO 3:

Let me be loving, even when it hurts me

RIO/PRABHAT - SOLO 4: Love will lead me to be at peace
CHORAL: Rise and Walk with Jesus and find Peace (2)

CHOIR: Rise and Walk with Jesus and find Peace (2)

KARNITA - ***NARRATOR 2***: Every time, we are tempted to sin, we trust God and 'Rise and Walk and Win.'

KASMIR - NARRATOR 1: Every time we fail and fall, we trust God and forgive those who hurt us, and 'Rise and Walk and Win'. We win Eternal Peace!

ISHA - BAHAI: I think Jesus teaches us, as individuals and as one big human family, to be rooted in God, deep within, and therein find our inspiration to 'peacefully', 'rise' and 'walk' into eternity.

A scene from 'Rise and Walk': Risen Jesus

ABOUT THE AUTHOR

Minino Allan S. Peter Tavares, sfx., is a missionary Priest from the Society of the Missionaries of St Francis Xavier (Society of Pilar) and a Physicist researching Acoustics and Soundscapes of Revitalising Sacred Spaces. His passion for theatre, music, and peace leadership, as a playwright and director, has been inspired by his own parents and has evolved into a cross-cultural theatre group that identifies itself as Shubh Sandesh Gospel Echoes.

Email: allan.wholysound50@yahoo.com

Made in the USA
Coppell, TX
03 June 2026

78262392R00080